Final Approach

My Father
and Other Turbulence

Mark Blackburn

CLARET PRESS

Copyright ©Mark Blackburn, 2023
The moral right of the author has been asserted.

Cover and Interior Design by Petya Tsankova

ISBN paperback: 978-1-910461-74-7
ISBN ebook: 978-1-910461-75-4

A CIP catalogue record for this book is available from the British Library.

www.claretpress.com

Take-Off

The games pitches behind the boarding houses on the hilltop were called 'Wilderness', for good reason. The boys were shepherded into position along the touchline by the Housemaster. And then we waited.

On this drizzly, sullen 70s day, out of the east a buzzing speck appeared and grew larger. It was a small helicopter, more a tangle of glass and tubes than any integrated machine. It was coming towards us, on the descent; no one knew who was inside. Its forward progress halted at the centre of the pitch. It hovered for a moment, the chopping whirr of the engine faltered, and the helicopter dropped slowly to the ground. The whine subsided, the blades slowed until they were individually discernible, then they too stopped. There was complete silence; the boys, the helicopter, the world. After a few moments, the side of the glass canopy cracked open, and out climbed a tall man in a long black coat with an astrakhan fur collar. My father.

The Housemaster stepped forward to shake hands. The other boys were allowed to disperse, and my father and I went to take tea with Mr Norwood. Afterwards I was told to fetch my things and then we went back to the helicopter. No crowd in formal attendance this time, although once I'd climbed in beside him and he'd started the engine, a steady flow emerged to watch our departure.

No sooner had we taken off than the low cloud curdled down to suck us up; the already poor weather was deteriorating. My father was no expert pilot, quite the opposite – he'd only just got his licence and this was his maiden solo flight. He had no experience of instrument flying. He flew by visual flight rules, and therefore was totally dependent on what his eyes could tell him, or in this case, our eyes. The cloud ceiling was about 500 feet, barely higher than the electricity pylons puncturing the skin of the flowing Berkshire countryside. All he could do was use the compass and head east, flirting with the base of the cloud while praying that he was above the wires and turrets, and able to react in time to any sudden rise in the terrain. I had instructions to watch out for these hazards, as well as any other craft also foolish enough to fly in the conditions, and any landmark that might help to guide us. Then I had to shout at him over the crackly intercom and tell him, the cockpit being too noisy for us to hear each other naturally despite being only inches apart.

He flew as slowly as he could without stalling the helicopter, a very basic Bell 47, just our two seats side by side in the glass bubble. The tension was as thick as the cloud, our progress negligible. Nothing familiar below, just field after field, lane after lane, the occasional higher ground or communications mast to swerve around. Then a miracle: we passed over a runway, the husks of three ancient helicopters, one of which was a skeletal 1950s Westland Dragonfly, ominously lined up at one end.

We set down on the grass on the other side of the tarmac strip. More by luck than judgement, my father managed to make contact with the control tower over the airband radio, and it turned out we'd come down at Blackbushe Airport in Surrey – at the wrong end of the runway away from the tower and the basic terminal. We'd already been incredibly lucky even to get to the airfield, and we were lucky that due to the weather it was closed, so there'd been no aircraft movements on the runway. Luckier still that a few staff remained in the control tower, vainly awaiting an improvement in the weather. My father fired up again, and under their guidance we taxied up the runway from our isolated spot and parked beside the terminal. Nobody said anything as we trooped in to report our arrival, but my embarrassed teenage self could tell they thought we were idiots who were lucky to be alive.

We sat there for several awkward hours in one of those lounges with furniture no one would ever buy for themselves – battered wooden foam-cushioned chairs with peeling covers and chipped coffee tables littered with aviation magazines. A couple of bored air traffic controllers across the counter listened to their crackling radios and looked out into the wet grey blanket. Would the weather break to allow us to take off again? It finally did; a mere ten minutes later we arrived at our original planned destination, Fairoaks Airfield at the other end of Surrey.

We swapped our seats in the helicopter for those of our waiting car, with me receiving explicit instructions to keep my mouth shut and let my father explain to my mother why we were several hours late home.

Every flight with my father should have carried a health warning, but I took no heed. Flights, literal and metaphorical, they were all risky. At that age, I had an excuse, I was still in the unqualified worship phase. I have less of an excuse for repeating the mistake in my adult years.

LHR

My flight to Cork's been delayed, just for a change. I'm sat at the gate in the new section of Heathrow's Terminal 1 watching the planes and drinking my mochaccino. I realise I could have been sitting in this exact location years ago, grid reference TQ 07764 75364, on the verge of my teens. Except then I wouldn't have been in the terminal. I'd have been on top of it, sitting on the roof of the Queen's Building, a seaside pier in the middle of an airport, and I'd have been holding a pair of binoculars, not a cup of coffee. Now I'm a businessman in my own right, amassing air miles on my travels. Trying to compete with my father? At least I chose a different trade – shoes not cars.

/

Back then, home was a ten-minute drive from Windsor, where my brother and I could get the 727 Green Line coach to Heathrow; the child fare was a few shillings. Either we'd walk a couple of miles to catch the bus into Windsor or pester our mother to take us there. She probably didn't mind, two preteen boys out of her hair for the day. My father would have been away, probably with that German mistress, all those years before we knew about her, on one of his frequent and often lengthy business trips. Maybe we were so interested in the planes because we thought they might bring our father back. Looking back, I realise I've always been a hoarder, trying to save the pieces of a lost childhood. I started collecting plane numbers to ascribe some sort of order in the world – if I could write down every number of every plane, everything would be under control, wouldn't it? It wasn't just the numbers. I had over a thousand airliner postcards.

We'd pack our kitbags, the most essential item a packed lunch: cheese sandwich, bottle of Cresta (it's frothy, man) and a banana, which made the cheese sandwich taste of banana too, especially if it was a hot day and we let everything mush up in the bottom of the bag. The treat was a Jacob's Club biscuit – favourite plain chocolate or mint, least favourite orange, though that was still okay. Every now and then you'd get one where the biscuit hadn't been inserted in the manufacturing process. Result, a solid block of chocolate, and life didn't get any better than that.

In too went the planespotter's tools: air band radio, log books and binoculars, to read the aircraft registrations. To misquote The Smiths, some numbers were bigger than others. Surprisingly, the Soviet ones were easiest to read, with CCCP 86607 or similar in big characters on the side of the plane, whereas an American airliner might have a tiny N747PA tucked up by the tail.

The radio was just a fall-back, in case we couldn't read the reg numbers or 'cops', as we called them. As in "Did you cop that number?" I suppose, when a plane flew overhead. Their mark-ings were also etched under the wings and sometimes visible even without the binos (by-nose) if the planes were landing over us. Once a year a specialist publisher issued a volume with all the airliner registrations listed, and our purpose in life was to under-line all the ones we saw, trying to fill up the book.

The radio looked like any other but alongside the usual me-dium and long wave you could listen to conversations between the pilots and air traffic control on VHF. So if you missed 'cop-ping' a number with the binoculars, you might hear the pilot speaking to the tower, announcing his flight details. If we got bored watching and listening to the planes – and I admit, we sometimes did, it could seem an age between one landing and the next – these radios could also pick up emergency service broadcasts. "Juliet Bravo, break-in at Thresher's off-licence, Great West Road…"

Fully equipped for our mission, we'd set off on a Green Line coach, but really just a single decker bus, which meandered up to Heathrow through Slough, Langley and Iver rather than the recently extended M4 motorway. Once we arrived, we'd go to the Queen's Building, the labyrinthine rooftop terrace straddling Terminals One and Two. Back then it was very simple – there were three terminals, One for domestic, i.e. within the UK, Two for European and Three for long haul. There may have been some discussion about a possible fourth terminal, but there was certainly no hint of a fifth one, and the idea of a third runway laying waste several nearby villages was still in the ether.

The Queen's Building was a throwback to a more innocent age, a seaside pier in the middle of the airport where the plane-spotters were outnumbered by friends and families waving off or welcoming travellers. Those expecting passengers would wait until they saw the right plane touch down, often under the guid-ance of a friendly spotter, and then they'd rush down to the ter-minal to be in place to greet their people before they'd collected their baggage and come through passport control. Now with the need for commercial use of every square inch of airport real es-tate and the disproportionate fear of a terrorist attack, everyone's insulated from the planes, except the actual passengers. They are spat out from or spilled into the fuselage of an aircraft they never even see the outside of, once they've passed through the snakes and ladders of the terminal escalators and walkways.

But as we passed whole days on the terraces, we lived and breathed kerosene. Not just looking at the planes, but revel-ling in the throb and rumble as the planes landed and took off. When landing, thrust reversers screeched as pilots urged their aircraft to a stop. Taking off they'd make even more noise, ev-ery inch of throttle needed to get a hundred-ton metal tube stuffed with hordes of people and their paraphernalia into the air. Nothing eclipsed the sheer thunder of Concorde, the afterburn-ers throwing flames as the albatross of a plane straightened its long-pointed beak and left the ground. The smell too – a perva-sive fug of burnt fuel.

Why the seaside pier as destination of choice for a young

planespotter? Well, it was all open to the elements, and there were little cafes and shops, and photo and recording booths. It was a rare day that we didn't take home a set of mugshots of us pulling faces or a cheap piece of vinyl recording some unlistenable din we'd made, loosely based on a current Beatles or Stones hit. There was a camaraderie among the planespotters, and if we missed catching a number somebody would volunteer the info. Happy days.

Happier days than those during term-time, anyway. We could still planespot, but it was… complicated. My boarding school was in the lea of Windsor Castle, on the flightpath, so that worked, sometimes. When the winds were westerly (they usually were), the planes took off over us, and passed too high for easy recognition. Either they disappeared into small black dots arcing their way across the Atlantic or skewered outwards to closer destinations. The planes ascended and descended into the wind to minimise the length of runway needed; a strong wind can halve the amount of runway needed for a safe touchdown. But sometimes on mild summer nights, in a light south-easterly breeze, the planes tangled with the turrets of the castle as instead they came in over us towards the capital. They seemed to fly so slowly as to question the laws of flight; flaps stuttering down, nose up.

The most significant obstacle to planespotting at school was a teacher, Mr B, who taught history and supervised rugby. He can only have been in his thirties, but was bald apart from a few long and wild wisps Bobby Charlton-style. He wore wire-rimmed thick-lensed spectacles. He didn't look the most frightening or threatening master, and apart from a large stomach, there wasn't that much to him.

History lessons were punctuated by the occasional piece of chalk, or worse, a board duster – a wooden thing about the size of a pack of butter – flying at me if I wasn't paying attention. I learned to sit away from the window so I wouldn't be tempted to look at the planes, but my inclination to drift off meant I still copped it sometimes, and I'm not talking about a plane number. I can't remember what I did to incur the standout punishment. During one lesson I upset him so much that he came and dragged me out from behind my desk, bundled me over to the large metal waste bin in the corner, picked me up and stuffed me head first into it, his hands around my ankles.

Still, it was safer with him in the classroom than on the playing field. On the rugby pitch he felt no need to disguise his bullying, and every instruction came with a punch or a kick. As I was one of the smallest, he made me hooker, the position right in the heart of the scrum where your sole purpose is to 'hook' the ball with your foot back out of the ruck, supported by a bulkier player on either side. I was rubbish at this, but it didn't stop Mr B. making me play there every game and getting angrier and angrier when I continued to mess up.

He hated planespotting with a vengeance, probably because it was an outdoor activity which required no physical effort whatsoever. Very bad weather meant no games, but it also meant "indoor play", so no watching planes either. One sopping afternoon, after a couple of hours playing Hot Wheels and reading War Picture Library comics, the rain stopped and the hardcore aviation enthusiasts (there were a few of us) snuck out to snatch a few numbers. We'd only been outside a few minutes when Mr B. stormed out.

"What are you lot doing outdoors?"

It was pretty obvious, and no one answered.

"It's indoor play, get back inside."

"But it's stopped raining, sir."

"I don't care if it's stopped raining, get indoors."

"Why?"

You can't question a man like Mr B. That pushed him over the edge, and he came at us, fists and feet, me the prime target, a Bash Street Kids cloud of whirring limbs, but with only Mr B. striking the blows. All perfectly legal of course.

I would wait until everyone had finally gone to sleep and hold on until the distinctive twin tail lights of the evening Pan Am 747 reminded me of something better outside, and I could sleep too. That plane probably wasn't bringing my father home, but I liked to think it might have been. Or maybe he was on another plane somewhere, going places and doing important things.

/

Finally, they call my flight to Cork; alongside my own shoe business which takes me further across the world, I cross the Irish Sea once a month to supervise one of my father's ill-advised side projects. Don't worry, we have a return ticket to Cork for an in-depth look at that later.

I've watched the planes, but I haven't heard much or smelled anything inside the anaesthetised glass bunker. Arthur Hailey wrote about Heathrow in his blockbuster *Airport* novel that it "is the kind of inefficient mess which only the English can create". He could have been describing Brexit, the English response to the approaching coronaviral contagion or any one of a number of contemporary fails. As for LHR, that never seems to change. I've spent hours and hours waiting here when the fog's descended or the wrong sort of snow has fallen, when air traffic control has gone down or all the airport computer systems have failed and no one can check in.

The place is perpetually on the brink of meltdown. But a third runway will apparently solve everything, just like a fourth or fifth terminal did – not. Notwithstanding the Covid blip, and with a continuing disregard for global warming, more planes fly than ever before, but I gave up trying to write down all their numbers a long time ago.

MIA

Holidays changed. Early on, they'd been on the south coast, a week or two in a small hotel or a rented cottage. Then, my father's fortunes improving, we bought our own Selsey Bill bungalow, down in West Sussex. We played happily with the coastguards' children, other locals and holidaymakers – normal kids, no school bullies to bust my nose (it wasn't just the teachers who were savage). We drifted from the beach to the caravan site fairground to the chip shop and back again, in no particular order.

But the south coast of England was no place to go in December, and as the bank account grew, the money pushed back the horizons. It also meant a whole new load of airports for us to discover, with their squadrons of exotic aircraft, registration numbers waiting to be noted in our logbooks.

One of the first holidays abroad was to Florida. I don't know if there were direct flights to Miami during the 70s; we certainly didn't take one. Despite his increasing wealth, my father never spent a penny more than he had to. Maybe the two are not unconnected, but he could be embarrassingly tight. Much more recently, I was in a cafe in Spain with him. Despite spending time there for forty years, he didn't have a single word of Spanish, so when he got one tomato on his plate instead of the two in the picture of the fry-up on the wall, he pointed at it and complained loudly in English. As usual he got what he wanted. Whether his second tomato had been spat on en route, who knew.

His carefulness with money meant our Florida flight left Stansted Airport in the early hours; first leg a charter to New York, then three hours on another plane down the Eastern Seaboard. That didn't bother me and my brother; fly one, get one free. First a big noisy four-jet engine Boeing 707 for the transatlantic polar arc, and then a twin-engine Delta Douglas DC-9 for the second leg. And three airports rather than two for looking at planes taking off and landing.

My father had a car business colleague who lived near

Stansted, Jack. His wife, Molly, was probably my first real-life crush. She had big red hair, wore only black and seemed very glamorous. They lived in a rambling house in the middle of nowhere, nearest town Bishop's Stortford. Snow lay on the ground. There was no heating in our rooms and I don't remember proper bedding – I think we slept in our clothes with coats and blankets on us. Maybe since we were getting up at about three thirty in the morning someone thought this didn't matter, it didn't really count as a proper night.

So one day between Christmas and New Year we got up very early and very cold, and left a snowy Stansted for an even snowier New York, where we stayed only long enough to catch the flight south. This was the shock of air travel. You could board a plane up an icy stairway and just a few hours later emerge into hot sunshine.

My memories of those teenage Florida holidays meld into each other, but sometimes we'd visit relatives in Fort Lauderdale. We spent a week seeing them and doing the tourist stuff – the Everglades, Disney Land or World, whichever's the Florida one. Mostly we were in hotels, days spent by the pool. With a mixture of distaste and admiration I observed what an operator my father was. My mother was only upstairs in her room reading, she couldn't take too much sun, and my father would be moving in on one of the shiny oiled women by the pool. They were closer to my age than his, but way out of my reach. I don't know what he was telling them, but it seemed to go down well. I couldn't believe it: my father the superstud, as Jackie Collins would have said at the time. I wouldn't have put it past him to start rubbing Hawaiian Tropic on their backs.

I don't know if he took all this any further, but knowing what I know now, it wouldn't surprise me. He'd have just told my mother he was going round the corner to the casino or something. She never seemed to be suspicious of him; if she was, she successfully hid her suspicions from us. I made the mistake once, by then a frustrated and probably in some respects jealous late teenager, of asking my mother if she didn't think his continual absences were just a bit odd. She was far from her placid self in replying, "How dare you question your father after all he does for us – and you?" The next mention of it would be years later in a Daily Mail article.

Back in Florida, we went to the cinema too – it was 1975, we loved airports, and guess what, we saw the disaster movie Airport. A 747 gets hit by a light aircraft rendering it pilotless. One of the flight attendants, Karen Black, manages to keep the plane in the air, but this being the 70s and her being a woman, naturally she can't land it, so Charlton Heston gets sent up in another plane and somehow dolloped into the cockpit to save the day. And all the passengers. Karen Black may not have been able to land the plane, but she did become my prime teenage fantasy interest; if only she knew. My brother said she was cross-eyed, but he was just jealous.

We loved it, but not as much as the real plane stuff. The second week, we took an ancient twin-prop Douglas DC-3 down to Key West. This plane could quite possibly have been an ex-troop carrier from World War II, under its military guise as the Dakota. Now it was operated by a little Florida airline, Air Sunshine, ferrying not troops into battle-zones, but overweight tourists to holiday resorts up and down the Florida Keys. It was a memorable flight, pretending to be aviation pioneers. The aircraft wasn't pressurised, so flew at a much lower altitude than modern airliners, flitting low over the coral reefs dotting the blue waters between the islands. The plane itself reinforced the sensation, bare metal panels struggling to keep the noise of the grinding piston engines from entering the cabin.

Even taking off was strange. Most planes have their wheels organised like an outsize tricycle – a nose-wheel and a set of wheels under each wing. The Dakota had a tricycle undercarriage too, but the wrong way round, with the third wheel at the tail. Starting the take-off run, instead of the usual sensation of the nose lifting, with the Dakota the tailwheel would lift first, so the plane levelled out before the plane separated from the runway. Only once airborne would the plane assume a more natural climbing attitude, though at a much slower rate of ascent than modern aircraft.

Key West was cool – I was just beginning to take an interest in stuff other than cars and planes, and reading books instead of Gerry Anderson's TV21 comic. We visited Hemingway's house and I lapped it all up; the writer, the big game fish, amazing sunsets. But what my brother and I were really looking forward to was our trip back up to Miami – to stay on our own for a couple of days in the middle of the airport, literally right under the control tower. We were going to plane spot until the rest of the family joined us from the Keys and we all flew home together to chilly Britain.

I can't believe now that they let us do it. The golden age of aviation was also the golden age of leaving your children on their own to fend for themselves, and not overly worrying about whether they'd succeed. These days people talk about *helicopter parenting*, taking an over-protective 360° interest in their children's activities. And as we've already discovered, my father clearly had a very different take on the concept of *helicopter parenting*.

I was midway through my teens and my brother was two years younger. Our father wasn't going to fork out for us to fly back up, so we took the bus all the way up the Keys, a spectacular journey hopping from one palm island to the next along a series of snaking bridges. If I was looking for help with detail from my 1975 diary, I wasn't going to get it. 'Left Key West by Greyhound. Arrived at Miami International about lunchtime', is all it says. We would have been alone on the bus for a few hours, with a couple of stops en route at the bigger islands. I do remember one about half way up being called Marathon. We had a toilet break there where there was a shop and we could stock up on supplies unsupervised, things you couldn't get at home – cans of lurid purple grape-flavour Fanta and corn candy, those little traffic cones of sugar-coloured red, orange and yellow.

When we reached the bus terminal, we had to find our own way to the airport. This involved a trip on foot across part of downtown Miami to get on the right bus route. I still remember how I felt waiting at the shelter: old enough to know that what we were doing was pretty out there, but young and naïve enough to not really be frightened. There weren't that many people on the street. Most of them had more sense and cruised by in their cars. We sat in the bus stop, not planning to reveal our chirpy little English public school accents. But a friendly old guy addressed us.

"Hey, what are you boys doin' here?"

"We're going to Miami Airport."

"You boys flyin' home?"

"No, we're going to look at the aeroplanes."

He chuckled. He took us in hand and made sure we got on the right bus. At the airport hotel, we had a room with a view looking out over the runways. I'm pretty sure we'd booked this in advance, though there was probably no need given most people would have wanted rooms away from the aircraft noise. We could monitor take offs and landings, and watch the planes and their tenders scurry back and forth on the taxiways from dawn to dusk. We didn't draw the curtains at night. Heaven.

From a planespotter's perspective, if there is a best airport in the world, it is probably Miami. Maybe not so much now, but forty years ago, MIA had the distinction of being the gateway to Central and South America, and therefore was the only place you could see in serious numbers the propeller airliners of the 40s and 50s, mostly retired from service in North America but still used in bread-and-butter service for the Latin American couriers. MIA was the dodgy nexus of the inter-Americas drug trade then and it still is now. Long after our stay there, Operation Ramp Rats saw nearly sixty people arrested after one sting operation which entrapped over forty American Airlines baggage handlers, ground crew and catering staff.

We could have stayed in our room and watched Lockheed Constellations heading off to Bolivia and Douglas propeller jobs carrying dubious freight to and from Mexico. These prehistoric workhorses run by exotic airlines like Aeronaves and Equatoriana were painted in bright oranges and greens, the colours of the perilous jungles they crossed (or sometimes didn't, they were old planes). These planes never visited Europe so they were precious trophies captured by our heavy binoculars. But we didn't stay in the hotel. Oh no. Because we couldn't see every plane in every extremity of the airport, we had to log them all!

However bonkers it was, we emerged from the safety and comfort of our hotel and set off around the circumference of the airport on foot, two skinny boys with our notebooks and cameras. We walked along perimeter fences and down access roads, popped through gaps and scurried into actual hangars, writing down all the plane numbers we could see, inscribed on the fuselage or under a wing. If no one seemed to be about, we'd get out the camera and take photos of the aircraft – 'numerous old crates and some biz jets', according to the diary.

A friend asked me what my brother and I used to talk about when we were doing all this. "Nothing" is the answer, we were brothers, what would we talk about? Well, nothing except planes. It was all-consuming.

"Pass me the binoculars."

"Can you read that number?"

"Wow, there's a Curtis Commando. First one we've ever seen."

"No one's about – shall we have a quick look in that hangar?"

Amazingly, nobody stopped us. Just one or two people asked questions, but when we told them what we were doing, there was just some head-scratching and they let us carry on.

We *owned* that airport. We walked every yard of it, captured every plane in it; we lived, slept and, in the terminal restaurants downstairs, ate there. We woke to the rumble of take-off, we fell asleep with the curtains open to the twangling stars of the runway lights. We'd have stayed there forever, or at least until the teenage hormones kicked in. But the parents showed up, and back to school in England for the rest of the long winter we went.

LPA

We didn't go back to Florida the next winter; we went to the Las Palmas in the Canaries for our dose of festive sun. It's pretty much the only place you can sunbathe in December without having to fly long-haul, as the Germans and Scandinavians had discovered well before us Brits, getting their towels down first. This is where the mistress got to see us, though we didn't get to see her. That became a regular pattern for us all: Florida one year, Canaries the next, lucky sods, until my father moved offshore with his girl-friend and the holidays came to an end. Eventually, he stopped coming back to the UK for Christmas, even.

The first trip to Las Palmas Airport I don't remember too well, although I can still picture men standing on the wings and sweeping snow off as we sat on the chartered VC10 waiting for it to warm up at Gatwick. Though I loved planes, I shared the collective fear that this icy, snowy plane might struggle to lift off the icy, snowy runway.

Our next trip there two years later is better documented. We were meant to leave on New Year's Eve, but my diary tells me 'fog halted play', and a couple of days later the family set out in two different parties, one from Heathrow and one from Gatwick. No doubt it had been impossible to rebook all six of us on the same flight after all the cancellations. Interestingly, rather than split up, my parents went via LGW with my littlest brother, leav-ing me the oldest to fly out with my other siblings! My sister would have had to put up with her older brothers banging on about aircraft constantly. It passed youngest bro by. As so often, he got left out, purely down to the age gap.

That might have been the only time the family travelled out on different planes, but it was standard practice for my parents to be up in first while we were back in steerage. In the event my father found himself next to a 'celebrity', he'd bring them back down the plane to meet us. Crackerjack! It's Michael Aspel!

On this trip, we all regrouped at Malaga, where we transferred onto the same flight to Tenerife. Here we got an island hopper for the final leg to Gran Canaria. Quite a journey, but great for the planespotting – according to my log, we got fifteen 'cops' at Heathrow, five at Malaga, eight in Tenerife, but only four at Las Palmas. Mind you, it was nearly midnight.

We joined the few Brits among the other Europeans. This was before the likes of Ryanair and Easyjet; UK visitors arrived on screaming four-engined jets capable of handling the four-to-five hour flight, VC10s (like the one we should have been on again) and Boeing 707s owned by charter companies such as Monarch and Caledonian/BUA, a merged airline which in turn was swallowed up by BA. French-built and Danish-run Caravelles brought in the Scandinavians, and the Germans had plenty of their own more modern charter planes to bring in their hordes.

The ultimate oil burner was the Spantax Coronado spewing its black entrails. This Spanish charter company had reprieved a fleet of American Convair 990 Coronados from the big scrapyard in the sky; smaller airlines would buy used aircraft from the major carriers as they neared their use-by date. We loved these big noisy, dirty buggers, not caring then about them rotting the atmosphere.

It hadn't taken us long to discover that Gran Canaria had its own microclimates, and often Las Palmas in the North East could be misty and dull while Maspalomas on the south coast baked in the sun. So we'd pile in the car – all six of us – and head off on a day trip. About half way down on the hour-long journey there was a massive black bull, an advertising hording for a sherry producer, perched on top of a hill. Dominating the landscape, this bull seemed to me to represent everything foreign and exotic. As we headed south I couldn't wait to see him loom into view, promising adventures far beyond the realms of our quiet English village and my even more removed rural boarding school.

Maspalomas means 'more doves' in Spanish, though I don't remember seeing any. What I do remember seeing among the sand dunes were all the naked bodies. Just beyond the main drag was a nudist beach. We'd no idea such things even existed. Now, right in front of us, was a comprehensive introduction to the varieties of human body. There was no clear delineation in the sand marking off the nude section. We'd wander a little further away from the car park, the bodies thinned out, and then those in evidence were clearly... naked! We'd get up as close as we dared to study the human form, new and valuable information for us closeted boarding school boys; filed away for later use.

You might not be expecting a ghost story, but here's one anyway. We didn't have a rental car like most of the other tourists – no, my father had blagged a beaten-up old BMW from his local counterpart, the Canaries importer. When we went down to Maspalomas, my father would drive the car as close to the sea as he possibly could, way beyond the tarmac and off across the sand and boulders, the BMW weighed down with the six of us and all our paraphernalia. Inevitably, there was the occasional grounding, and after one particularly big thump to the undercarriage even my father was uncertain if the steering was still fully functional. As he pondered the wisdom of driving back up to Las Palmas after our day on the beach, miles from any garage or even firm road, a BMW service van turned up alongside, the big blue and white rondel on the back. My father's luck.

Anyway, the mechanic had a look at the car and sure enough, the steering linkage was hanging by a thread. We could have all been killed if we'd tried to drive back. Luckily, he had whatever he needed in the van, fixed the car, and we were safely on our way.

Next day, my father mentioned to the car trade buddy who'd lent us the car the fortunate encounter with his mechanic. The guy was puzzled – he knew nothing of any such person. He was the BMW agent for the whole island, and he didn't have such a van or employee. Despite further enquiries, we never found out where this engineer had materialised from, or what he came to be doing amongst the dunes in the middle of nowhere. Whatever, he fixed our car.

We didn't learn of her existence for another twenty years, but my father's girlfriend, Ursula, was coming on these holidays too. We found out courtesy of the Daily Mail. They ran a regular feature titled 'The Secret Rich', and the spotlight fell on my car dealer father and a German woman I'd never heard of let alone seen, described in the article as his partner.

After this bombshell, my father, who NEVER called, summoned me to meet him and this 'partner' at a Heathrow Airport hotel as they passed through (it had to be at an airport, didn't it?). At the meeting a few days later, my three siblings and I met this woman who took pleasure in telling us how she'd been coming on family holidays with us – the 'us' including our mother. This other woman was shacked up in another hotel – or was it the same hotel, just on another floor? Ursula, who therefore must have been with him at least twenty years without our knowledge, didn't tell us that, though she did tell us how she'd watched us as kids, playing on these sand dunes. We'd all been under her close surveillance; even my mother sitting there reading one of her Georgette Heyer novels.

Wherever Ursula was stashed away at night, my father would venture out to see her when he was supposedly on business or off fishing, or when he went off 'to the casino' in the evening. Where she was the day of the breakdown, who knows; maybe she had her own car to follow us around, or on this particular day perhaps she was back sunning herself by the pool on the roof terrace.

There was no hint of all this going on as we enjoyed our holidays, and our parents indulged our planespotting. Although designated LPA, the actual Aeropuerto de Gran Canaria wasn't near Las Palmas but half way down the coast to the south. We'd pass by on our trips to and from Maspalomas and stop there for a drink or a meal on the terrace. It was a small airport then, an attractive art deco building from 1930 with a balcony restaurant and cafe looking right over the apron, perfect for spotting. It had been built as a stop off on the new route from Toulouse to Casablanca, when aeroplanes could only fly a few hundred miles before needing to refuel. Of course, it's gone now, ripped down in 2014 to make way for a larger modern terminal, despite being a 'building of historic interest'.

For us, the airport had something else going for it: it was also Gando Air Base. The military airport shared the runways with the civilian side, but had its own hangars and administrative buildings over on the eastern flank, where the camouflaged Spanish Air Command fighters and bombers lurked tantalisingly beyond the range of our binoculars. It was busy with operational traffic too, notwithstanding the domestic volatility during the final days of the Franco regime. When we visited activity was at its most intense post-war, principally due to the Spanish decolonisation of the Western Sahara and its ensuing occupation by Morocco.

We did once set off on foot to explore these extremities but decided it was too hot and too far, and rarely perhaps common sense prevailed as we realised poking around military planes was probably not a great idea under a totalitarian government. That didn't stop us taking long-distance pictures from the terminal or trying to catch their numbers as they taxied to take off. Not for the first or last time we were probably lucky not to be incarcerated, unlike the thirteen British and Dutch planespotters who were jailed for six weeks in 2001 for taking photos at the Kalamata air base in Greece, another military facility shared with a civilian airport.

LPA is infamous in aviation history for another reason. The worst ever civil aircraft disaster took place not at Gran Canaria Airport but because of it, while we were still going there as a family. In March 1977, the airport suffered a rare terrorist attack – a bomb was planted in the florist's inside the terminal building by a movement attempting to secure the Canaries' independence from Spain. A ten-minute warning was given, and despite a number of injuries, no one was killed in the attack.

But in the ensuing airport closure, air traffic was diverted to the smaller Los Rodeos airfield on Tenerife, including several big aircraft on long-haul flights. The smaller regional airport struggled to handle the extra influx and the larger planes. Jets had to use the taxiways to park on, and the runways to taxi on. In a terrible chain of events, just as the airport was most congested, a thick fog fell. Despite this, and air traffic control being unable to see the planes, aircraft movements continued. A KLM 747 commenced its take-off run, but crashed into a Pan Am Jumbo taxiing along the runway. All 583 passengers on both planes died, the highest ever loss of life in a civil aviation accident.

Our final family visit to Las Palmas happened that same year, my last teenage Christmas, all thoughts of terrorism and disaster already melted by the eternal sunshine. I've no idea whether Ursula was lurking along the coast or along the corridor that time. We did the usual stuff: the pool, the dunes, and I got myself a good tan for my second term at college. Not very street cred for a student wannabe punk-rocker, granted; I think that's when I christened myself Rhino Surfpunk.

What sticks in my mind most from that final trip was a funny little coincidence right at the end of it. There was a Spanish guy I'd met in France the previous summer during my gap year. He'd given me the lyrics to the Moody Blues' Nights in White Satin, which he'd written out painfully and decoratively in his finest longhand. I suppose he had a bit of a crush on me, though as I was sleeping with a different girl every week by then (we'll come on to that), I didn't pay much attention. Looking back at the lyrics now, I guess there's not actually much doubt:

> Just what the truth is
> I can't say any more
> 'Cause I love you
> Yes I love you
> Oh how I love you

(Justin Hayward, © Sony/ATV Music Publishing LLC, Universal Music Publishing Group)

Sorry, Antonio, I never took the hint.

Although I'd given up writing down numbers by then, I still liked watching planes, and while we were waiting for our flight home to Gatwick I was back on that terminal terrace having a beer in the late afternoon sun. Suddenly Antonio appeared at my side – he'd been here on holiday with his family too. Six months and a thousand miles apart, and we both end up in the same airport cafe. It was an unlikely encounter, and he probably thought Fate had played its hand and bestowed great significance on our reencounter. But no, that was that, and we never saw each other again. That's the sort of thing that happens at airports.

BBS

At Blackbushe on the last day of July 2015, four of the Saudi Arabian bin Laden family perished when their Brazilian-made Embraer Phenom 300 business jet overshot the runway and smashed into the British Car Auction site at its end. The weather was good and could not be blamed; the plane had apparently landed too far down the runway after avoiding a microlight aircraft on approach. Despite its modest size, Blackbushe calls itself an airport rather than airfield, and has had more than its fair share of disaster. In 1957 an Eagle Aviation Vickers Viking crashed there with the loss of all but one of the thirty-five on board, and a year later, the year I was born, a Royal Navy Seahawk broke into pieces in the clear blue skies above.

There had been no such fine weather that day I came closest to an airborne death, as my father's first ever passenger as a helicopter pilot all those years ago.

/

I later boarded at Bradfield College near Reading, a much happier place than my hellish prep school. Despite one of my friends there warning me I'd be going from the frying pan to the fire (I could imagine my feet being toasted over hot coals) Bradfield turned out to be a much more civilised and humane place. I think too I'd prepared myself better – I pretended to be less of a nerd than I really was, and dressed as trendily as school rules allowed; wide lapels, regulation dark grey trousers flared to the max and Cuban heels on my black leather shoes. I got away with it, despite a faux pas on the very first evening when I called a prefect who turned the dormitory lights out 'Sir'. It didn't even enter my head that this man who looked so much older than my squitty thirteen-year-old self wasn't a master.

My father's behaviour could be a risk to my welfare too. While other boys were delivered to school or picked up for half-term breaks in the family Volvo or Peugeot 504 estate, my car-dealer father would have something to prove with the latest exotic vehicle to pass through his showrooms – a Maserati Ghibli roadster or a stretched Mercedes 600 Limousine, the sort of car you'd more likely associate with the Pope in the early 70s. While the petrolhead teenager in me enjoyed the sports cars enough to suppress the cringe reflex, the pink Cadillac convertible was too much. It was more painful because at the same time my father was going through a particularly exhibitionist period, quite possibly as part of a midlife crisis. He'd emerge from these cars wearing rakish hats and Russian fur coats, sporting a wad of facial hair across his upper lip. Consider all of this was very close to the time of the fuel crisis and the three-day week and you'll understand he wasn't your typical dad.

I've flown in and out of Blackbushe with my mother too, in very different circumstances. While they were still together, horseracing was one of the few things my parents still enjoyed in each other's company. My father's car business was flourishing, and it can't have been long after the helicopter incident that they bought their first racehorse. Now that I think about it, my father had met Ursula, his German mistress, by then. Still, it didn't stop him buying a horse with my mother. Helicopters were involved in this too – they'd fly off to race meetings from the paddock at the back of our house. I suppose the helicopter was just one logical step up from the flamboyant motors.

They say horse racing is a mug's game, and most owners never win a race, but true to my father's extraordinary luck (he would say sound judgement) this horse turned out to be fantastic. It was a stallion called Gloss which won several top races. Pundits know it from being involved in an infamous photo finish at Royal Ascot involving the Queen's horse – all the first three were disqualified, though I remember that the sentiment in our camp was that this had been a gross injustice.

Gloss won a race in York, the Nunthorpe Stakes. It must have been during the school holidays because I was there and got to meet the Queen, who presented the prize. I can't believe that now. It feels as if I'm writing about a different person, not myself, but the picture's there to prove it. Me with Her Majesty, and I'm still in trademark flares and wide-lapelled jacket, with a pair of enormous shades; Britt Ekland would have been proud. In a couple of years I'd turned from squitty and skinny to lanky and skinny.

Despite his intrigues with other women, this time probably marked the high point of my parents' relationship. They had their shared passion for horse racing, we still went on trips together as a family, and my father was at home more often than not – just about. The family continued to congregate for Sunday lunch, even if my father's golf partner that morning meant an extra place setting. But not long after this, he became estranged and started living abroad with Ursula. For the first twenty years of this arrangement, my mother kept up the pretence that this was all perfectly normal, and Daddy was away all the time because he had to be, because of the tax man. I smelled a rat; I knew so-called tax exiles were supposedly allowed in the UK for up to 90 days a year, and we saw far less of my father than that. However, my protestations were slapped down.

Even after all this, or maybe because of it, both my parents pursued their interest in the turf, my father more expansively. He blew ever larger sums from his increasing fortune, while my mother continued more modestly on the allowance she received from my father.

Eventually the increasingly-exorbitant odds turned in his favour, and he went on to win one of the biggest National Hunt races there is, raising the bar so high that he's been unable to repeat his success. He's tried harder and harder to do so, ratcheting up his frustration and significantly diminishing his bank account.

My mother stuck to flat racing, having been hurt by the loss of a horse over the hurdles early in her time as an owner – I know, the horse suffered a lot more. But she's also had more than her fair share of success, and that's where we return to Blackbushe.

Her best ever horse ran in the late 1990s, and was a filly called Eveningperformance, all one word to fit the Jockey Club requirement for a name not to exceed eighteen characters. EP, as we called her, was one of the best sprinters in the country, probably the fastest horse of all over four and a half furlongs. Unfortunately, the shortest races are five furlongs. Nonetheless, she won some highly rated sprints, with no one catching her as she began to fade on the final approach. Hence she was deemed good enough to travel to France to take part in the sprint race at the Arc de Triomphe meeting, Le Prix de l'Abbaye.

My mother had shown no interest in any other men, even when my father's behaviour had been exposed, and as the oldest son I'd become quite used to being the fixer, on hand for occasional 'official duties', like accompanying her to Red Cross functions (she was a County President), race meetings and the like. With a party of eight (the trainer and his wife, the stable jockey, my mother, my wife and I) going to Longchamps and back for EP's big day, my aviation knowledge came in handy. I'd pointed out to my mother that rather than buying eight return air or train tickets from London to Paris, it might be cheaper (and certainly easier) to hire a plane for the trip.

My father doesn't have much faith in me, but my mother believes I can sort out just about anything, so usually I do. This time I did my research, and found a twin-engined Piper Navajo operating out of Blackbushe.

The Arc de Triomphe meeting takes place on the first weekend of October, which is often blessed with very fine weather. Our big occasion was no exception, and we took off on a warm, sunny morning in our 'rubber-band job', as my wife called it.

It's a much more engaging experience of flying in a small unpressurised plane, feeling the vibrations of the propeller engines through your seat, having a big window to yourself and being tossed around by the skittish clouds. Indeed, by the time we landed at Le Bourget just to the north east of Paris, it was high in the 70s. I'd arranged a minibus to take us round the north of Paris to Longchamps, and all went smoothly; as we taxied up to the terminal, the bus was there, out on the apron. Border controls don't try too hard with the privileged, I've noticed.

We had a grand day out, being wished good luck by Clare Balding (then Channel 4 Racing commentator) and Andrew Lloyd Webber, even. Eveningperformance had a great run, doing the usual and leading into the final furlong, when she faded. Still, she came in third, which put her in the prize money and paid for the plane rental.

Anaesthetised by champagne to the hot-air turbulence, we flew back to Blackbushe in the Navajo, bearing if not a scalp at least a plaque for being placed. We crossed low over the channel into the fine autumn sunset, not a cloud to be seen. Unlike the damp day many years before when my father couldn't even see the end of the runway, now the airfield lay below us, glinting like a giant Scalextric track in the late afternoon rays. We floated down to a soft landing, taxied to the terminal and all was still for a moment as the pilot cut the engines. I can't deny it; at times, I've been a lucky bugger.

AGP

Today's flightplan takes us to Malaga, another outpost of the Blackburn family empire. I'm on an Embraer 190 narrow-bodied jet with just four seats across out of London City Airport (LCY). As we approach our destination, the wingtips flirt recklessly with the dark crags of the Sierra Nevada. Jewel blue pools encrusted with glittering sand nestle between the peaks, tempting a passenger to dive from an emergency exit straight into them; a teasing trailer for the Mediterranean, just now visible beyond the ridge.

The rise and fall of hot air over the slopes cause the plane to pitch like a sports car leaping over a humpback bridge. Then, relieved to be across, the engines sigh as the power dips, the mountains left in their wake as the plane describes a gentle arc over the sea. Now on one side there's only turquoise water, and on the other the Battenberg cake building blocks of the Costa del Sol, merging into the horizon at each end. Then the final approach to Malaga Airport, the waves slapping below, ever closer to the fuselage.

Sea gives way to sand, and to the left, or should I say on the port side, are the apartments, where I've been coming for forty years.

My father, increasingly paranoid and therefore increasingly hostile as he spills into his eighties, has made this his European base, and he would usually be down here during the summer months with his entourage, including his official partner, Ursula. When his acquaintances meet me they often assume she's my mother; I try to correct them politely. I call her 'partner' because no one's quite sure if he's married to her or not – he might be according to the statutes of a Caribbean island-state, but certainly not according to UK law. And 'official' because there's also an unofficial partner, Mandy from the Wirral; trim, blonde and half his age. Ursula is a mere fifteen years younger than him, and was the original long-term replacement for our mother. Did she ever want her own children? We'll never know; sadly she developed Alzheimer's. As a result, there are also two nurses taking it in turn to look after Ursula, the whole ensemble travelling together. Completing the troupe are my father's driver and his husband. The driver, Charles, only a few years younger than my father, had been chauffeuring him most of his life.

On this trip however my father and his entourage aren't here. He's repaired with most of the clutch to his even more temperate perch at his home in the Caribbean, leaving Charles and Mario to mind the hacienda. Mario, real name Agron, an Albanian hotel manager from Eastbourne, is half Charles's age, with knowing brown eyes, sharp cheekbones and an even sharper intellect. It's an unlikely match, but it seems to work, and he doubles up as a minder for the whole crew. I'm very fond of them both.

The purpose of this visit is to carry out family business, but my father has started to believe that I'm "trying to depose him and take over". The latest piece of evidence supporting this growing conviction is his belief that I didn't tell him about this trip. He's wrong; he'd even phoned me to discuss the fax I'd sent with the details (yes, he was the last man on earth using a fax machine). No point in arguing. Because of this though, he's forbidden Charles from driving me. Our relations are souring. We've had sulks and silences before, but this time the decline seems inexorable. Where will it end?

After I pass through the glass and metal maze that has replaced the big concrete shed of the old airport, I look forlornly for Charles the driver anyway, hoping there might have been a last-minute softening in the curmudgeon's attitude.

But I've read my King Lear, I should have known better, and there are no familiar faces in the arrivals concourse. I find a taxi instead, and pay a small fortune to be driven the thirty tortuous miles to the villa along the Costa Del Sol. It's one of the most dangerous roads in Europe, today made more so by the winter winds off the cool Med, buffeting the lightweight panels of the flimsy cab.

At the hacienda I meet Charles and Mario, who are embarrassed at being forbidden to collect me. We go for a pizza and bitch about the old bully, then they drive me (ignoring their orders) virtually all the way back to the airport, to the Parador de Golf, a seaside hotel and golf course a stone's throw from those familiar apartments *they* are now staying in. I go to my room and it is as if the room had been specially chosen for me, looking straight out on the flight path. As I open the blinds an executive Learjet with a vivid orange paintjob squeals over me on its finals.

Charles and Mario are due to pick me up again later (still against orders) to take me into Malaga for a meeting with our lawyer – nothing contentious, just a catch-up taking care of family matters, checking progress on various little disputes. Whose obligation is it to maintain the well? Who owns the car park area at the back of those apartments? Stuff like that. But I have an hour or so before we have to leave, so I walk out into the gardens bordering the golf course to get some air. Not only can I watch the planes, I can see the apartments across a small river struggling to carve its way through the sand to the sea.

/

My father bought those apartments nearly half a century ago, but I don't remember my mother ever coming here. She probably never did, as he seems to have bought them as a bolthole to slide off to with Ursula. She certainly wasn't around the first time I visited. My father wasn't around either – I can't remember why, but my brother Stephen and I had been despatched there during one summer holiday to stay with Tim and Tash. Tim was Charles's predecessor as his driver, and Tash was Tim's wife. Maybe it was because our parents thought we could spend a week harmlessly planespotting from the apartment balcony.

There were two flats next to each other on the top floor of a three-storey block. My father kept the larger' one locked up for his own use, and the four of us were in the smaller one. Both flats were pretty basic, but ours extremely so. I suppose they were bought before my father got mega rich, but even when he had money, he never spent money on stuff like 'decor'. A second-world-war upbringing and spartan public school dormitories had left their mark. Remember too that this was the early 70s, and the whole package holiday phenomenon was in its infancy. Charter flights were only just taking off, as it were. Our flat had no running hot water, the floor tiles were cracked and ill-fitting and there was damp seeping through the plaster in most of the rooms.

But it was a superb place to watch the planes. These were the days of very noisy jets with shallow flight paths, and we'd have plenty of warning one was coming, as it screamed in over the sea. We'd rush out onto the balcony with our binos, which here we barely needed, to see the registration numbers on the side of the planes.

We would have happily camped out on the balcony all the daylight hours, although there were some long gaps between the planes. We'd peer out to sea waiting for the next one, and then tease each other mercilessly when one of us mistook a seagull or a flyaway balloon for an approaching jet. However, all was not well in the land of Tim and Tash. They'd argue loudly, but the paper-thin walls gave them no privacy, so to escape our confines we'd all pile into the car hidden in the tiny basement garage and make a sortie.

If the flat was a bit crap, the car certainly wasn't. It was a lovely little silver BMW convertible from days when German cars still had a bit of personality, and which my father had got hold of through being the UK importer. The best thing about it was the 8-track player, with a small but perfectly formed collection of cassettes, mostly Beach Boys and Beatles. Roof down, volume up, we'd drive along the coast road and up into the hills thinking we were the business. Tim and Tash didn't seem to mind; it saved them from having to talk to each other.

Our fixation with aeroplanes being insatiable, we'd noticed while driving through one village that it had an excellent panoramic view of our airport below. We persuaded the two Ts to take us up there one day, and we found a little cafe with a terrace looking down across the runway. We sat there and drank orange fizzy pop in old-fashioned bottles with pressurised glass stoppers. We made it last as long as we could.

From our vantage point, we were thrilled to spot a plane we hadn't seen coming into land from our usual balcony spot. Parked away from the terminal but therefore close to us was that most rare aircraft, an executive jet. This was before every sanction-busting, tax-avoiding global megacorp worth its salt mine had a fleet of business jets, and this North American Rockwell Sabreliner – even the name sounded exotic to our young ears – conjured up all kinds of possibilities. What sort of person could possibly own their own jet, and what was it doing here on the Costa Del Sol?

At some point later on, we found out Tim had a gambling problem, and quite probably that had been the source of the marital strife. The holiday came to an end, my brother and I returned to our family, still nominally intact, and my father got a new driver, Charles, who was living in those selfsame apartments forty years later.

During my later journeys down, I admit I'd try to avoid my father. I didn't need to feel like the clumsy awkward child I'd been when he disappeared in my early teens. I tended to regress in his presence. On one trip though, he'd been part of the reason for my visit. He'd given clear instructions regarding the 'gifts' I was to bring – a bottle of Scotch (had to be Bells), some bacon (had to be streaky) and the latest copies of the Country Life and the Daily Mail (he used to be a Liberal when I was young, but I couldn't imagine him reading my Guardian). You wouldn't think these items would be that difficult to buy in Spain, but those were his orders.

I got the bacon before I left home, bought the rest at Gatwick with the whisky duty-free, stowed it all away safely away in my carrier bag and then of course left said bag in the overhead locker. I remembered before meeting him on the other side of customs (he had at least come to meet me, certainly not a given) but then I had to go back to the plane, against the flow, and deal with all the officialdom on the way. I did manage to retrieve the package, but that meant I was last out into the arrival's hall – a cardinal sin in the Blackburn Scheme, where being the first out was paramount. My father was waiting in an agitated state. I had become a useless teenager again, and that tone was set for my visit.

Another time he arrived to meet me with his latest girl-friend in a tiny Mitsubishi convertible. This girlfriend was a Romanian con artist, and that's stating it mildly. Magda cleaned him out for a tidy sum approaching seven figures before she cashed in. She preceded the current model, Mandy, and was about half Mandy's age and twice her bra size.

The little Mitsubishi (he'd made an even bigger fortune importing Japanese cars after his success with German ones) didn't have a proper rear seat and I had to sit sideways in the back with my knees sticking up – all six-foot-three of me. Of course, the roof was down, so everyone could see the prat in the back. Unfortunately, this went on for the entire visit, as we toured the various family property and business interests.

It sounds pretty grand that, and I don't want to pretend I haven't had it good, very good. I've always felt a disconnect.

I know, and do appreciate, that I've had all the benefits. But sometimes it's felt like it's not the real me that is experiencing them, it's as if an alter ego is, and the real me is watching it all happen. Through my binoculars as a planespotter? Taking in my helicopter view? It would be ridiculous to pretend that I'm not extremely privileged, but I still feel grounded in the soil of my grandparents' tiny little rural house with its outside lavatory. They were both below stairs in service, and now I'm very much on the other side of the divide. But if I'm not working class, I don't feel, and never have felt, that I fit naturally into the world of regattas, golf clubs and polo matches.

So sitting in discomfort in the too-small back seat of a multi-millionaire's car feels entirely par for the course. My father at ease in the driving seat, his long legs stretched out in front of him to the pedals, while I'm at the point of nausea, legs scrunched up so if my knees had eyes, they'd be peeking over the back of the parcelshelf.

/

Whatever. After twenty-five years of selling shoes (more on that soon) and trying to be my own man, I got sucked back into this opulent mess. Next morning, Charles and Mario came to pick me up at the hotel, each of us having sworn to silence regarding our harmless deception of the old man. I saw the lawyer, I saw the accountant, I visited the properties and I watched the planes come in over the sand, landing lights blinking against the Mediterranean sunset.

ABZ

I've only been there once, but after forty years I still hold a deep resentment against the ground staff at ABZ. I didn't intend to use the airport at all, but circumstances forced my hand.

When I reached the sixth form, school became a much happier place. We had a lot more freedom, and we started to meet… girls. I wasn't a great singer, but I wasn't a foghorn either, and I blagged my way into the Choral Society, purely because they put on joint productions with Downe House, the girls' boarding school a ten-mile bike ride away. In the last few weeks before a production, we got to perform together, a coach bringing them to us, our music school probably considered better than theirs – if they had one.

She wasn't one of the best singers either, I don't think she'd mind me saying, but I fell in love with Helen, who was doing anything she could to escape the confines of her oppressive school. She was beautiful – ash blonde hair and cloudy grey eyes; tall, slim and much posher than me. Her family were landed gentry, whereas mine were perceived by such folk as tres nouveau riche, my father being a mere car dealer. But we clicked: we both had a rebellious streak, we liked the same music and we sent constant letters to fill the gaps between choral practice and the weekend bike trips between our schools. By summer 1976, the hot one, we were definitely 'going out'. I'd gladly cycle for an hour over to hers, and boys were allowed a brief visit on a Saturday afternoon, as long as it was in the common room and in the safety of numbers. Sometimes she'd bike to Bradfield with her friend Christina and we'd slope off with bottles of barley wine into the long grass beyond the Wilderness playing field, the staff at my school being more relaxed (not that I wouldn't have been in deep trouble had the booze been discovered). Our finest hour was managing to attend Newbury races in my friend Stirling's bright blue Mini – somehow he'd managed to secrete it on the premises during his last term, an 'engineering project'. Our fantastic foursome ticked off all the rules we were breaking – the car, cigarettes, alcohol, the opposite sex and gambling. A full house.

The summer holidays arrived, and the prospect of eight weeks apart was too much to bear. So we decided I'd go and visit her in Shetland where her extended family owned one of the whole islands and then she would come with me for a week to our more modest holiday cottage on Selsey Bill.

The heatwave had broken before the glum wet day I took the train north from Kings Cross. Still, I was very excited – my first trip to go and stay with a girlfriend. I hadn't travelled that much on my own, usually going places with our big family or with a pack from school.

All went well until we were somewhere bleak and exposed on the Cheviots north of Morpeth; the train just stopped. No clanking, no grinding – nothing, and then silence except for the rain driving against the windows. We waited for a few minutes and then we waited for a few more minutes. An announcement. The train had broken down. We waited for an hour. I didn't panic, I had left a few hours buffer at Edinburgh for the connection to Aberdeen. Another announcement – they couldn't fix it, another locomotive was coming from Newcastle to rescue us. This took another hour or so, and it became clear I might not get that connecting train after all.

Big deal, just get a later one, I thought. Well, no, I soon found out. The later train was much later, and the point about the train I was booked on was that it met the Aberdeen to Lerwick Ferry. Which ran only twice a week. Not only that, but a whole chain of interconnecting smaller ferries to the smaller Shetland Islands fed off the main one. So if I missed my connection, I wouldn't see Helen for another four days, and my holiday would be ruined.

It was grimmer than that. She and her father were due to meet me outside the Grand Hotel in Lerwick, close to the ferry terminal, at 10.30 the next morning, and then we were going to drive back to Fetlar (the family's island) via Yell, Unst and the small ferries in between. Of course we didn't have mobile phones then, but worse still they didn't have a phone on Fetlar! There was no way I could tell them I wouldn't be on the ferry.

I just had to get to Lerwick somehow in time to meet them.

As expected, the train limped into Edinburgh well after the Aberdeen service had gone, and the next one *was* too late for the ferry. Nonetheless I took it, it got me that much closer.

Once in Aberdeen, boats were obviously out of the question now so I found a bus to the airport, which wasn't too far out of town. It wasn't much of an airport then, though I expect oil money has tarted it up since. There was just one big shed, which had everything in it – ticket desks, the check-in, toilets. Not much else. There were no flights out to Shetland that evening, and there were no scheduled flights out the next morning, certainly not in time for me to make the rendezvous with Helen and her father. However, I poked around and discovered I could buy a ticket on an oil company flight heading out to Sumburgh, the airport on the Shetland mainland, early the next day. Now there was another problem. Money.

I had some cash on me, my spending money for the week, and it was just enough to buy the air ticket, which was pretty reasonable – about £60, from memory. This might just work after all – the flight was at 8.00 the next morning, and got in just after 9am.

The seating in the departure lounge was pretty sparse and basic, but I could manage one night on it. Not much of an ordeal when you're used to iron beds in school dorms and tents on the Brecon Beacons. I put my bags down, my feet up and closed my eyes. I woke up only about an hour later to find my bags had gone. Of course, I thought they'd been stolen, but only for a moment. I looked round to see I was being given the evil eye by some uniformed types.

I went over and asked them politely if they'd seen my bags. The grumpiest one pointed at them behind a counter and told me to take them and get out of the airport, loitering was forbidden. I tried to explain my predicament, but they just sneered. I suppose in the summer of 1976 they would have been unimpressed by a tall skinny English youth in the midst of his transition from Bowie freak to punk rocker, but still. There's mid 70s customer service for you.

So an extremely miserable lanky streak of a kid trudged back along the road towards Aberdeen to try and find a cheap hotel for the night. I had very little dosh left, but my first worry was getting out of the rain.

I found a hotel soon enough, on the periphery of the airport, but it was full; there was a wedding reception going on, with most of the guests staying over. I started to shuffle out again, when I heard someone telling the desk clerk they wouldn't be staying over after all. The kindness of the receptionist as she called me back made up for the tossers at the airport.

Now came the tricky bit; the bill. The nice woman let me ring my mother, who managed to pay my bill on her credit card, something eighteen-year-olds didn't have in those days.

I could have done with double the sleep, but adrenaline shortened the early morning return hike to the airport. The flight on the oil company Vickers Viscount left on time, and there were no delays. What I hadn't reckoned on is that the airport on Mainland is at Sumburgh, the other end of the island from Lerwick, nearly thirty miles away on bendy single carriageway.

I shared my challenge with the taxi driver (another friendly person!) and he pitched in, clock and meter ticking in competition as we rallied our way north. I got out of the taxi in front of the Grand Hotel at exactly 10.30am, and had just enough money left for the fare. Watching me get out were Helen and her father. He started to give me a bollocking for lazily taking the taxi the short distance from the ferry port, though he quickly softened when he heard my tale of woe.

Helen's parents were titled and quite elderly – I worked out her father must have been about sixty when she was born. Despite a certain reserve they were gentle and kind. I did upset her father once, by pulling the outboard motor out of the water to slow down the little boat we were pootling about in when I got into a spot of bother. It stopped the boat alright, but it would have been simpler and a lot less noisy to just switch the engine off.

I'd like to say that we had a wonderful weekend together, our relationship prospered, I got the ferry back to Aberdeen as planned, and in a way, that all happened. Nevertheless everything went awry when I was discovered in Helen's bedroom after her parents unexpectedly returned home early from an outing. We were only playing chess and listening to Supertramp. To be in her room wasn't the crime of the century, but as her mother kindly and sadly explained, one just didn't do that sort of thing in that sort of household, and as a result Helen was banned from the return fixture with my family.

I returned to Bradfield for one more term during my gap year to do Oxbridge exams, and Helen went to Rome. We met a couple of times more, but Aberdeen was the final destination as far as our relationship was concerned.

WID

"If you like planes so much, why didn't you become a pilot?"
Good question. Long answer.

/

Planespotting at school did ramp up my interest into an obses-
sion, but aircraft appeared on my radar even before that. Two
of my uncles, my father's sisters' husbands, were in the Royal
Air Force, both officers – one was a helicopter-flying Squadron
Leader, and the other a high-ranking Air Marshall Sir of the
Realm. The knighted one was also my godfather. Christened
Leslie, he was known as 'Duke', a more appropriate soubriquet
for a military bigwig. Although he normally flew a desk, certainly during my childhood, there were often aircraft-related treats
on offer – a flight in a glider, aerobatics in a Chipmunk trainer,
circuits in a big Hercules troop carrier, Boy's Own stuff. One
time Uncle Duke gave the salute at the Royal Tournament at
Earl's Court, and had me alongside him in the royal box.

No surprise that when I had to choose which branch of the
cadets to be in at senior school, aged thirteen, I chose the RAF.
At my prep school, I'd watched the planes thunder in overhead
and grabbed the registration numbers from their wings, but now
I could get up close and personal. There were actually two other
options – you could do the Duke of Edinburgh's Awards, or you
might end up in what was called the Pioneer Corps. But to do
the D of E, your parents had to really push for you not to do
the military option, and that was never going to happen in my
case. The Pioneer Corps wasn't something you *chose* to do either
– it was for boys who were considered unsuitable for anything
else. They had to do forced labour – clearing the river, weeding,
rubbish collection. No thanks.

So every Thursday afternoon I had to put on my scratchy
blue serge uniform and do boring stuff like endless drill or

terrifying stuff like the assault course across the river. Once a term all the cadet branches united to do 'arduous training', hiking across somewhere like the Brecon Beacons with a full pack on your back. To my surprise, this I could do well. I had a deserved reputation for being rubbish at games, and when we all traipsed off from Tal-y-Bont reservoir one freezing December, everyone thought I'd struggle. But I was a little Duracell bunny among the bigger rugger buggers. As they started to flounder on the hills I reeled them in, and was one of the first back to camp. Who knew I had stamina. A life of long-distance hikes and running marathons lay ahead of me.

But for all the drill and exercise, plenty of what the Air Cadets did was aviation related, culminating in an attempt each summer to actually fly – in the school grounds.

I can hardly credit it now, but in a shed at the end of the playing fields there was a DIY glider. It was like an enormous Airfix kit that the whole Air Force corps would unite to assemble. Its only saving grace was that it wasn't made of balsawood. There was one main two-dimensional fuselage piece, and all the other bits, wings and all, were bolted on to this. Safety clips on each bolt were supposed to ensure they didn't fall out. 'Supposed to', bearing in mind a random selection of teenage boys was inserting the pins. There was an elementary seat fastened to the front of the structure for the pilot, leaving him exposed to the elements and more significantly any frontal impact. Think Kate Winslet on the bow of the Titanic, only in blue serge and wearing a beret.

So far, so implausible. But now we come to the method of propulsion. Once this oversized piece of Meccano had been assembled it was dragged by the boys to one end of the sports pitches where it was secured to something, I think the tow-bar on a Land Rover. Then an enormous catapult was produced – a massive Y-shaped piece of elastic. The foot of the Y had a hook in it, and this was fastened to another hook on the front of the glider. Then two teams of boys would each take an arm of the Y, and they'd stride away from the aircraft, on divergent paths. At some point the officer in charge, i.e. master, would decide that the elastic was sufficiently tense, and the order was given for the catch on the Land Rover to be released. The glider would jerk forward, and then slither at speed on its runner (part of the fuselage, no wheels) between the two lines of boys. When it had reached sufficient velocity, for just a few yards it would leave the ground, and the terrified pilot would have the sensation of flight – no, he'd have the reality.

I only remember being the pilot once, but of course I remember it well. As with any other aircraft, there was a joystick, and to make the plane lift off you had to pull it back, but the most important lesson was not to pull it back too far, otherwise you would take off alright, but the nose would come up too high without sufficient speed and you would stall, thus crashing the glider and at the very least injuring yourself. When it was my turn, I did what most people did, and pulled it back so gingerly that I flew only a couple of feet above the ground, and for not many yards. Still, I did get airborne, and not everybody managed that. It is a wonder that nobody ever did get hurt, and I suspect my generation was the last to benefit(?) from such a relaxed attitude to health and safety.

My cadet experience culminated in a week-long 'field trip' to a real Air Force base, RAF Wildenrath in the Rhineland. Wildenrath was one of four RAF 'Clutch stations' built in northern West Germany after the Second World War, as part of the general Allied effort to avert a repetition of German military ambition. We didn't actually fly into Wildenrath, which had no customs clearance facilities, but into nearby RAF Laarbruch, which did. We flew on a chartered BAC 1-11 twin jet from Luton. I remember getting off to a bad start when I tried to find a check-in desk for the flight – there wasn't one. I was supposed to report to someone somewhere and then become a part of the troop. Eventually I must have worked this out, because I got on the plane. We arrived at Laarbruch in the middle of the night, and all piled onto a coach to Wildenrath. Good value for the planespotter in me, even if it was dark and most of the hardware was in the hangars.

I didn't get any flying experience at Wildenrath, but I got about two years' non-academic education in a week. The cadets on the field trip weren't all from Bradfield; they were from half a dozen schools across the UK. There was one contingent from Hulme just outside Manchester – these guys were secondary modern pupils and quite unlike anyone I'd come across before in my sheltered decade and a half. My primary had been a state school, but in rural Berkshire. These Northern lads were hard, but they were kind, and all the japes were directed upwards; there was no bullying. Us posh kids were taken in hand, and when there was a midnight attempt to kidnap the station mascot, we were allocated support roles; St Custard's newbies gophering for the criminal masterminds. The sortie failed, and we were caught 'out of bounds', but apart from a good bollocking and some extra drill, we were let off – they could hardly send us home early.

Wildenrath was home to the VTOL (Vertical Take-Off and Landing) Harrier fighters, and they were never going to let us near those. But there was plenty of up close and personal plane stuff, and time spent in the hangars. There was some non-plane cadet action too: one night we were taken to a point in the middle of the German countryside miles from the base, and told to find our way back, so my newfound stamina came in handy. When the week came to an end, I felt a lot more confident and independent, which soon came to bear fruit.

Leaving school for university, the family intention was that I'd go for an RAF flying scholarship, where they paid to put you through college on the understanding you'd sign up afterwards. It was expected I'd join the air force or become an airline pilot or do both, so it made sense. The bible of application forms arrived, and I diligently filled them in. Without giving it any thought at all, while smugly ticking the 'no' box against all sorts of ailments and conditions, I did allow myself a 'yes' tick against the hay fever question.

And for that reason, I was automatically rejected. My god-father was furious; why on earth did I mention the hay fever? I'd given no thought to its significance. Quite reasonably, the RAF might not want someone flying a Lightning jet at 700mph a hundred foot above the ground to have a sudden sneezing fit.

Without a scholarship any flying lessons had to be paid for, and my father did fork up. After I'd worked a summer in France and before I started at the London School of Economics I did an intensive course over a month in a tiny single engine Piper Cherokee at White Waltham, another ex-Air Force base a ten-minute drive from home. My girlfriend at the time, Silvia from Frankfurt, six foot and sinewy, whom I'd met in Nice (where we'll be touching down later), had come to stay. Though my interest in most things re planes remained undiminished, I did find my interest in recording all their log numbers diminishing in direct proportion to my increasing interest in more worldly attractions. We'd drive over together and she'd curl her long legs up on the tiny back seat of the Cherokee while I was being taught. Luckily, she liked planes too; she soon became an air hostess for Lufthansa. My instructor, Jamie, wasn't much older than me, and had wild long red hair, a beaten-up black leather jacket and a beaten-up Triumph Spitfire he'd lend to me and Silvia to go to the pub between lessons, while he took up other pupils. I stuck to drinking Coke.

I took to the flying like a duck to air, and after three weeks, by which time Silvia had gone back to Germany, Jamie said to me, "Right, you can fly the plane now." I thought he meant he was just going to sit there and not touch the controls, but then he began to climb out of the aircraft. There I was, on my own, taxiing towards the grass runway. I mechanically followed the drill, lined up on the runway, put on the brakes, pushed the power up to full, released the brakes, held the plane straight as it accelerated along the grass and gently lifted the nose when I reached the appointed airspeed. I was flying! On my own! For a few seconds, I did wallow in that. Then I realised that whether I was ever on the ground again and still alive was down to just one person – me.

I watched the airspeed and climbed steadily to the set level for the anti-clockwise aerial circuit around the White Waltham. I headed west until I bisected the London-Bristol railway, and then I turned a slow one-eighty back towards the airfield. Seeing it pass by on my left, I joined the sweeping final approach down over the trees, taking care not to get too close, and all the while slowing down to the required 85mph for landing, but making sure I didn't let my speed falter beyond that point, where I'd stall the plane and fall out of the sky. Trees avoided, there was the runway right where it should be, in front of me. I gently raised the nose so the wheels would be the first part of the plane to encounter the ground. They did, more or less smoothly; I was down.

Though I flew solo a few more times that September, I didn't get my pilot's licence. I failed the aviation law exam (probably too much time crashing out with Silvia) then university started and I lost the motivation to do any more exams than the ones I had to do to scrape through.

I didn't want to be a pilot anymore. I could escape my earthly self in other ways. I could see a wild mutation as a rock-and-roll star. Or maybe as a stand-up comic – Adrian Gatwick was waiting in the wings. I still had a tendency to hoard and collect (I still have, though it's more under control) but back then I collected every single piece of David Bowie vinyl I could lay my hands on, bootlegs including Live at Nassau. My obsessive behaviour became channelled into finding the platform boots with the highest heels, the loudest jackets with the widest lapels.

My aeronautical inspiration, Uncle Duke, died soon afterwards, but not before he was knighted. My own flying aspirations became derelict, much like RAF Wildenrath.

After the Berlin Wall came down, the need for a major RAF presence in what had been West Germany became redundant. On 1st April 1992 the base closed down. No April Fool's joke for those who worked there; the last remaining contingent, 60 Squadron, whose main purpose was troop transport with no offensive capability, moved to nearby RAF Bruggen.

Bruggen itself merits a paragraph for being the site of a nuclear incident which could have wiped out the whole of Europe. In 2007 the RAF admitted that 23 years earlier a nuclear missile had fallen off a truck on one of the taxiways because it wasn't secured properly. Obviously, it didn't go off! Bruggen was only returned to the German authorities in 2015, and is now used as accommodation for refugees.

As for Wildenrath, part of the airfield has been taken over by the industrial giant Siemens as their rail test centre; now railway tracks interweave with the old runways. Much of the remainder has just been left to be used by the locals in whatever way they see fit, while another section has become a golf course. Fore!

MUC

My father could never be like other fathers and would never be like other fathers, so my family could never behave like other families. Most of the posh ones at school had a Jaguar or a Bentley, the solid upper-middle classes had Volvo or Peugeot estates, but being a mega car trader, mine had foreign exotica like Maseratis and Mercs to suit his extrovert extravagance. A BMW coupe got christened the Flying Saucer by some wag. When four wheels weren't good enough, however flash, my father arrived in that helicopter.

So true to form, instead of flying home on the RAF charter flight with the other cadets from Wildenrath, I had to do something completely different. I wasn't going back to Luton, but flying down to Munich to join the rest of the family for Easter. By now my father had bought an apartment on Starnbergersee, a picturesque outpost for München's wealthy half an hour south of the city towards the Alps. In theory this was his bolthole near the BMW office and factory, but no doubt really his love nest with his German girlfriend Ursula.

It was my first flight as an 'unaccompanied minor' and I took full advantage of flying alone. When the drinks trolley came round, I ordered a beer. I still remember the stewardess (let's fess up, we didn't call them flight attendants in the 70s) and her reaction. She was the German stereotype I'd imagined my father's mistress to be before I met her – a thirty-something blonde who'd look equally at home juggling frothy steins in a bierkeller. She was surprised but also amused at this English boy asking for a beer, and she served me a can of Lowenbrau with a smile. I had another one, but didn't push it – the flight from Dusseldorf to MUC was only an hour. Nevertheless I came out of the baggage claim nicely squiffy and very pleased with myself.

That was one of the few trips we made to Germany as a family – usually my father went on his own, most weeks it seemed. But we did make another that summer – to the 1972 Munich

Olympics. BMW was probably one of the sponsors given the company HQ was a four leafed-clover of a tower overlooking the Olympic stadium.

It was the games where terrorists shot and killed eight Israeli athletes. I kept a typical teenage boy's diary and it's extraordinary now to read my simplistic coverage of those horrific and unforgettable events. It's also extraordinary to see how little difference it made to the progress of the games, and our participation as spectators in them:

August 31st – Went to Athletics and saw David Bedford do well.
Sept 4th – Arabs killed Israelis in Olympic village.
Sept 5th – Went to Olympic wrestling. Went to cancelled football.
Sept 8th – Went out with Tim and Tash first to Olympics then to the shops.

I always think of my mother as a worrier; I wonder how she felt about all this? But for my father, the show would have *had* to go on. I do admire that in him.

The final family visit was winter two years later, when I was sixteen. Since I could remember, we'd had au pair girls, though for some reason we didn't call them that – they were always the 'mother's help'. Clearly at my age I didn't need bathing and putting to bed, though I was getting to an age instead where I was very keen to attract the attentions of an au pair. That said, my little brother was still only eight, both my parents worked and that's how we rolled. Seven of us when we travelled, and that was without the occasional driver/relative/school friend in tow.

Our final 'mother's help' was Lizzie, who was only ten months my senior, and I fancied her painfully. She was from the West Country, and had very long dark hair, big brown eyes and a figure I couldn't ignore. She was about a foot shorter than me – I'd grown about that amount in the previous two years. On the journey out to Munich, she was wearing a tiny stripy green and white halter neck top, spray-on bleached jeans and strappy platform sandals. My father must have come straight from his office because at Heathrow he told her she wasn't travelling with us looking like that.

I remember there was a big row. Lizzie was more stroppy teenager than adult, and she often gave back as good as she got – my father was no exception. But she lost on this occasion, and sulkily compromised by putting on a sweater over the top.

There were two apartments next to each other on the Starnbergersee, with my parents being in one and the rest of us in the other. Every night Lizzie and I used to stay up late and horse around, the frolicking developing from arm to body wrestling, just stopping at the point of anything overtly sexual. I was desperate, and though I think she was pretty keen, she restrained me with promises of teaching me stuff just before she left. She did go within the year, but sadly I never got any lessons from her. I was probably away at boarding school when she went.

Through my teens I continued to love cars and I still do, I can't help myself, despite a snowflake guilt over my carbon tyre tracks. But I came to dislike the motor trade. Perhaps subconsciously I held it responsible for my father's absence, and anyway, I was turning into a glam rocker and then a punk, which didn't sit comfortably with the boorish motor trade and flash cars. I determined that whatever I did with my life, I didn't want to follow my father into the business. Ironic then, that my love of running led to a part-time job in a trainer shop, which led to a career in the sports trade, whose European epicentre was... Munich. But more of that later.

My father might still have been entertaining thoughts about me joining him in the car trade though, and thought learning German would be useful, so I was sent to stay with Familie

Holzner in a suburb south of Munich for a month. It was evident that the more wealth and power he accrued, the more my father expected his own family to fall into line like the cronies he surrounded himself with in his newfound glory. "Never argue with your bread and butter" became a favourite expression, somewhat at odds with his earlier philosophy that his children's individualities and personal attributes should be encouraged.

Herr Holzner was a greengrocer with a stall by a U-Bahn entrance, and lodging language students was an extra money-making scheme for the family, nothing more. Outgoings were minimised to preserve the profit margin. Meals tended to be whatever fruit and veg was left over from the stall – I remember plum pie being a staple on many evenings, and that was the main course. The place can't have been very clean either. I caught a bad dose of crabs from my bed. That might have been to do with the further economy measure of not changing my sheets for a whole month. Hopefully they'd changed them before I arrived, but thinking back, I'm not entirely sure. I wasn't being precious, I'd have changed them myself, I had done so every week for seven years in boarding school, but that wasn't an option.

It was a lonely month because the language school was a long commute from the Holzners and had no social hub to it – students came in, used the labs during the day and went home again, in my case to a cold apartment where there was very little going on. There were two Holzner sons, the older one having the sense to spend as little time at home as possible. The other one, Peter, was a couple of years younger than me and becoming awkward and unhappy. We did have one good evening out, at the Oktoberfest where we got pissed and went on some rides, but Peter earned a beating from his father when we arrived home late and drunk and was grounded for the rest of my stay. The paying guest avoided punishment.

A few days before I left, I had to reconfirm my flight home, so this was an excuse to leave the flat and go to the airport and look at some planes. I wasn't very confident about reconfirming over the phone anyway, and the Holzners weren't about to give me any help.

Reconfirming your flight is another bygone aviation custom now that we book everything online – hard to believe nowadays, but if you didn't reconfirm, you were very likely not to get on the plane. It was common practice to overbook every flight so the airlines ensured they didn't have any empty seats, confident that there'd always be a couple of dropouts. If you didn't reconfirm, you might get bumped off.

I set off to the airport armed with the tools of the trade – my binoculars and air band radio. I thought I'd get the business end dealt with first and then look at some planes. No problem, I went straight to the airline desk and had reconfirmed in a couple of minutes. I wandered across the terminal to find a viewing area. Three armed German policemen came into view, and merged to form a black, glinting wall in front of me.

"Wo sind ihre papiere?"

I got out my passport and air ticket.

They looked closely, and noticed my flight wasn't departing for several days. They pointed this out, their interest growing. I used my three-and-a-half weeks of German to try and explain that I'd just reconfirmed my flight.

Wondering why I'd needed to come to the airport to do that, they demanded to see inside my bag. Seeing the binoculars, they became very excited, and I was off to one of those little rooms they always have in airports but 99% of passengers never see. I've been in them far too often; serves me right for looking like a scruff/drug dealer/smuggler far too often in the last forty years. Now the skinny English teenager (me) was removing his cheese-cloth shirt and flares for inspection by the burly polizei. Thankfully it wasn't a full body search and after about half an hour's questioning and a good look at all my planespotting stuff they let me go, satisfied that there was no clear and present danger but finding it bizarre that anyone would want to do this. Strangely, I didn't really feel like watching planes after that, and slunk back to my infested cell at the Holzners to see out the last few days of my sentence.

As it turned out, I didn't get to use my German in the car trade, but a few years later I was making business trips to Munich as a shoe buyer.

Before the onslaught of the Evil Empire (as Nike was known by some in the business) and other American brands, adidas and Puma were the biggest players in the market, sales driven by their dominance in the football industry. Not only did adidas and Puma originate from the same country, they emerged from the same family (and note it's always adi with a small 'a', whatever Windows tells you).

The Dasslers made football boots for Germans, but the two brothers fell out. Adi Dassler kept the main business, and brother Horst went off to found Puma. For a long time they were the protagonists not just in Germany but across Europe. Consequently, the industry trade fair ISPO took place in Munich. Despite my best attempts, every six months I was breathing my father's exhaust fumes anyway. I could so easily have bumped into him and Ursula, years before I knew that was even a possibility.

But I loved my Munich trips. The sports trade then was an exciting place to work – my company profited from the booming popularity of marathons. Then two trends combined to make trainers even more fashionable. First, the European football influence. British fans would travel abroad to watch their teams play in Euro competitions, and would buy or steal the most obscure 'kicks' possible to wear with their tracksuits – the Puma Vilas, after Guillermo, the tennis player, the Patrick Copenhagen, the adidas Trimm Trabb (don't ask me to explain that one). There was even the adidas Kick – whether that related to kicking balls or people, I'll leave with you.

Second, the Americans invading with their funky runners and basketball hi-tops, doing a grey squirrel on our poor old Green Flash. Our little shops were well poised to take advantage of both trends, and for a few years we coined it.

And I was one of the first sneakerheads in the country. When fashion mags wanted to borrow trainers for photo shoots, they came to me, and I got to do interviews in style bibles like The Face and appear on TV talking about footwear trends. There were good parties – I remember Naomi Campbell was at one in Munich, though I can't pretend she so much as looked at me.

So twice a year I flew in and out, looked at shoes during the day and partied most of the night, a bar called the Nachtcafe being our after-hours hub. The sports trade turned out to be as macho as the car trade, but there were enough fashionistas around to give it some colour and drag it cursing and kicking into the twentieth century. Now hipsters fight over the latest Yeezy Boost by Kanye West, and celebs like Rihanna and Stella MacCartney do collaborations with Puma and adidas. What would the Dassler brothers think of all this? And Munich being at the European heart of it all.

During the time I've been flying out, the city has had two different flughafens, both with the same IATA code. On our trade trips we'd fly into Munich Riem, but as with the world over, that airport became too small for the city's visitor numbers, and a larger, grander airport had to be built further out, with a grander name too, Franz Joseph Strauss Airport. Towards the end of my retail tenure, that's where we'd fly to. More travel time, higher transit costs. An improvement?

The old airport, Riem, closed down and became an exhibition centre. Guess where our ISPO trade show moved to? Now instead of walking miles of terminal gangway, I was walking between miles of product displays – in the same buildings. Quite odd to think that as I sat in an exhibitor booth writing out orders for thousands of pounds of trainers, I could have been in exactly the same place twenty years earlier being given my going over by the Polizei.

I've sold up and got out of shoes now, so I don't go to MUC anymore. There's no family reason to either, as now Ursula's worsening Alzheimer's has assigned her to a nursing home in gentler, warmer Spain. My father's traded her in for a new model. It's what happens in the car business.

ORK

So here I am finally. Cork must be the only airport whose IATA (International Air Transport Association) code has been formed by taking away the initial letter, that is, O-R-K, ORK. It would be like calling Oslo SLO or Nice ICE. Ireland must have been at the back of the queue when they were handing out the codes. I've been flying to ORK most months for what seems like forever. Fifteen years ago the job I had in Newcastle came to a sticky end and, seizing on my availability, my father asked me to work for him. So now I'm looking after family interests in County Cork, among other places.

As I've now moved from London to Somerset I'm heading there from Bristol (or should I say, BRS) for the first time. We're in an ATR twin-prop, slower than the Boeing jets out of LHR, and the journey will take longer, despite it being half the distance.

/

When I started doing my monthly sortie to Cork some years ago (all those sinful air miles), I flew from Stansted on Ryanair. It was guaranteed to be grim – tiny rigid seats, no leg room for my six-foot-plus frame, but the more convenient Aer Lingus out of Heathrow was prohibitively expensive. Even if there was load-samoney splashing around in the wider family, it always felt right to me to get the cheapest flights, same way I'd rather get a bus rather than a cab. Then, with Aer Lingus steadily going bust, the fares came down to match Ryanair. I could justifiably switch. It wasn't just for convenience. Quite apart from the scrum to get on a Ryanair plane, on one trip the young flight attendants couldn't close the door, and the ground staff had to return and climb back up their ladder to assist.

When a small start-up called Jet Magic began flights from London City Airport in 2003, that was even handier. They used small twin-engined Brazilian Embraer 145s, and as so few people used the service it was like having your own private jet.

But while the service was indeed magic, the passenger numbers didn't increase, and barely a year later the airline pulled off the ultimate disappearing act. The Cork airport owners seized one of their planes for unpaid landing fees. Many lost out as Jet Magic were still taking bookings just thirty minutes before they ceased operations; I was one of the lucky ones. Such a shame, it was a really friendly little airline. The marketing can't have been good enough, the secret was too well kept.

We cashed in on our London house as the prospect of continuing work for the family was looking precarious and my father and I were becoming more and more at odds.

I should have known better. I'd worked under him before and that had ended badly too. I was kidding myself that this time it would be different. That we'd revert to the effective father-and-son team I felt we'd been when I was young, and I'd sat there in the passenger seat while he road-tested the latest exotic European supercar he'd brought home for the weekend. That he would trust me to be his genuine partner, rather than just another serf.

Initially I'd had the sense to avoid the car business with him and made my own career in retail – first at the Virgin Megastore and then at a chain of running shops. I started out as the part-time van driver to still have time for my music. Then I realised that my new wave band was no more than a very small ripple. I went full-time into retail and ended up as a director soon after my 30th birthday. I used to kid myself I'd be a millionaire in my own right before I was thirty (yeah, as well as a rock star and a movie idol), but company director wasn't bad, in the five or so years I'd been doing a 'proper job'.

I had a foot in both shoe trends of the time. The jogging boom meant everyone was buying running shoes, and trainers had become high fashion. Business boomed and the chain grew quickly. As Buying Director I was responsible for purchasing millions of pounds worth of shoes and clothing a year.

Then we tripped up, big time. In the financial crash of the early 90s, the bank which funded our expansion had become insolvent, and was sold for a pound. The bank's new owners wanted their money back. We couldn't pay it. We'd opened a unit in just about every shopping centre sprouting up, and too many of them became ghost malls. We still had to pay the rent, even if we had no customers.

We needed a saviour. Well, I knew someone who had money. My father. Never mind that by now I only saw him once a year, in the run up to Christmas. Not for Christmas itself, you understand – he had other plans for that. We'd be treated to dinner at some hotel or golf club on a convenient date (for him) the week before. I hardly ever spoke to him otherwise. I didn't even have a phone number for him or know where he lived. Still, I knew how to get a message to him, 'in case of emergency'. Maybe this wasn't exactly an emergency, but surely in the circumstances it was worth it?

Now, I'm not actually sure that it was. He did save the company that November, he bought it for £1 (those days saw a lot of transactions for the sum total of a pound) but then we just teetered along for the next five years, with him drip-feeding dosh to cover cash flow crises and no real investment in the fabric of the business. Some years were better than others, and he did have the chance to double the money he'd put in when an offer came in to buy the company after we'd had a good year, but he turned it down. He wanted to wait; he thought one day it would be worth tenfold, not double. He was wrong. In March 1998, just after my 40th birthday, I had to call in the administrators.

I had found a new formula for the shops, widening the offer to outdoor and more fashion. The pilot scheme was a massive success, sales doubled and we were rolling out the concept, with my father's sanction. He was finally going to put some investment capital in.

Problem was, the money didn't materialise to pay for all the new shop-fits. There was another financial downturn, even his car business struggled, and he pulled the plug on us.

Despite the success of the new format, he blamed me. Probably it's right I shoulder some of the blame. Maybe I wasn't tough enough or focused enough. I was a great Buying Director, with an eye for fashion and the right blend of flair and caution, but perhaps not such a good MD. Most of all, I should have stood up to him more – as in all things, he thought he knew best, and for too long I thought he did too.

/

Even after all that, I was dumb enough to go back for more. So now I'm approaching Cork airport in very low cloud, conditions which would have meant a diversion just a few years ago. With modern technology a plane can land in all but the thickest fog, which is no rarity here. Often the pilot has announced halfway across the Irish Sea that we're off to Shannon, and buses would be there to take us on to Cork. Since Clonakilty, where I visit, is between the two airports this arrangement doesn't make much sense for me, and I wait at Shannon for someone to pick me up; have some lunch or do some work.

This time though I'm relieved to see the rooftops through a momentary break in the cloud – we're going to at least attempt a landing. You can never be sure until you're on the ground. Occasionally the pilots come down, don't like the look of it, and scoot off to Shannon. That was one of the few advantages (or not) of flying Ryanair – they seemed to be less fussy than other airlines and would put the plane down whatever. You'd see an

Aer Lingus 737 bang on the power in the gloom and overshoot, heading off to Kerry or Shannon instead. Then ten minutes later what looked like the same type of plane but in Ryanair colours would come in and land.

As more houses become visible, I notice we're on a flight path I don't recognise, even though I've flown into Cork a hundred times or more. We're not coming in over the craggy coast-line due south, indented with the likes of Roberts Cove and Ballinclashet, and we're not passing over the rolling farmland to the north. We're very low over the city itself, approaching from the east.

I'm sure nobody planned it that way, but this is after all Ireland, and even the airport is in the shape of the cross, the spine of the main runway running north to south with a tiny crossbeam east to west. I've seen light aircraft from the flying club use the shorter one on summer days when I've been sitting in the terminal waiting to fly out. I know we're not on a large jet, but surely we're not going to land on that?

Then the familiar airport buildings come into view over to my right, the wrong side, and I can see that we are. There's a lot of buffeting too; we're heading into strong westerly winds, the dregs of Storm Henry. This will be an interesting landing.

It is. Ironically the high wind makes it safer to land on the short runway, slowing us up more quickly, but the wings pitch to and fro just feet above the runway. At the critical moment the pilot steadies the plane and the wheels touch down more or less together. There's an almighty din as the thrust reversers are engaged to brake us harder and the plane judders to a halt. It looks like we're just yards from the end of the runway, though I'm sure we're well within 'operational limits'. I realise after I've written this how crazy that sounds – this isn't a jet, how can you reverse the thrust on a propeller aircraft? By controlling the propeller pitch of the prop, that's how. A pilot can effectively make the prop push the air in the opposite direction, thereby braking the plane.

We taxi in and come to rest by the old terminal. During the time I've been flying here, they've built one of those identikit massive new terminals, all metal and glass, but there's been some longstanding dispute between the airlines and the airport operator, and they hardly ever use the air bridges, those tubes from the plane straight into the terminal, except in the very worst weather. I'm sure someone could explain it. Today it's just the usual damp and breezy, so we disembark on foot and make our way across the tarmac to a long-covered walkway to the new terminal.

I travel light, hand baggage only – I've spent too many hours of my life waiting by luggage belts – so I'm one of the first out of the airport (Father would be impressed), and as usual Taigh is there to meet me in an old Mitsubishi, one of many in Ireland and another relic of my father's motor trade days.

No sooner have I told Taigh excitedly about the use of the crossbeam runway than he brings me down to earth with unsettling news. At some point in the last year or so, as well as my father deciding I'm incompetent, he's decided I might be dishonest as well, so he's sent one of his old cronies from the motor trade to spy on me. This bloke's been snuffling about just a couple of weeks before my visit, and Taigh had the dubious pleasure of driving him around.

Taigh never misses a trick, and we're barely out of the airport car park when he asks me if this fellah will be working with me. I know this is designed to extract the backstory, but I'm quite happy to put him straight regardless – I wouldn't work with the duplicitous slime bag in a hundred years. It turns out Taigh has a similar opinion, but was just testing the water. Over the next couple of days, I have my usual meetings with managers and agents. The place is falling down and the so-called commercial activities there – farming, gardens and golf – are haemorrhaging money, so it needs to be sold. My father holds this against me too.

It's a beautiful country estate on the banks of the River Argideen, "Silver Stream", replete with nine-hole golf course, farmland and gardens open to the public. But it's falling into disrepair. I'm not sure if it's more depressing to walk around the house or the gardens. The truth is the place has always lost money and there's never been any investment.

Builders are in, tarting the rooms up before the hoped-for sale. I say 'hoped-for' – it's been on the market for a couple of years now, at a 'top-dollar' (another of my father's favourite expressions) price, which no one is remotely tempted by. Damp is sneaking in everywhere. Ripping off the plaster shows the cracks in the old beauty's make-up. The conservatory, built for the Cork Exhibition a hundred years before and painstakingly moved here, is now a broken web of rotting wood holding up cracked panes, many of which are missing. One more heavy storm could bring the whole fragile structure down in shards.

The dignified library holds the same books that the shelves supported a century ago, but a constant hum keeps me company while reading there. The electricity fizzes and buzzes as the round plugs of the older wiring fight with the square pins of a patch-up job. The tired pipes shudder and groan at having to push water around the old house. The more expensive works of art have already been sent for auction, replaced with dodgy landscapes by obscure artists.

Stepping outside gives some relief, for a moment. The gardens are still beautiful in the early evening sunlight, but closer examination re-instils a sense of loss. Small pot plants pretend to fill spaces where statues have vanished and fallen trees straddle the river, their branches birthing new islands of gravel and weed. I try to navigate the paths which constituted my regular circuit, but give up when I can't even determine where the path ought to be. The place needs someone with deep enough pockets to gild life back into it. I hope the sale goes through.

Before I leave, the housekeeper tells me that the crony was asking her if I could have been stealing jewellery and paintings. I don't know what makes me feel more sick – his blundering in and suggesting such a thing to good people who've been working alongside me for sixteen years, or the fact that my own father put him up to it. Do I hold back a tear at the thought my own father thinks I'm a thief? No, it's buried too deep. Maybe one day I'll cry, but for now I seethe quietly inside. The remains of another day.

When I fly into Cork during the winter there's always a worry the weather will stop me flying out again, and I certainly don't want that to happen after this depressing visit. One year, for four straight months November to February my flights had major disruptions. Serious flooding – a one-hour detour to avoid roads, even whole towns, deep under water. The flooding's even worse now factory agriculture and development have reclaimed the peat bogs which soaked up that infamous rainfall. Snow – we nearly missed Christmas back home in London. Black ice – the runways closed. Fog – waiting for it to clear, sometimes days. The airport is built up on a plateau, so when the cloud comes down low, as it often does in Cork, it suffocates the runways.

This early February day is masquerading as spring, however, and the hop across the Bristol Channel is in glorious sunshine. The Worm on the Gower is poking his head out into the Atlantic, and the fingers of the bridges across the Severn estuary rest gently on the sparkling water. I take back twice as much luggage as I went with, my bags crammed with my father's jewellery and paintings (not really). I'm starting to bring my own things back, clothes, books and stuff, because I know I won't make this journey too many more times.

GLO

Gloucester Staverton, or as it's rather more grandly known now Gloucestershire Airport, was the nearest airfield to the HQ of my father's car import business, which he'd fly into from wherever most months for board meetings. The current plan was to meet him and his entourage there after one such meeting and fly with them on down to Nice. We're going to discuss the potential relocation of his horseracing activity from Spain, where there's little turf action, to France where it's obviously much more established. Currently I'm still in favour, more or less; my ability to speak French might be of some benefit, my father doesn't speak a word being of the persuasion that the whole world should speak English. Besides, I'm looking forward to a return to the Cote d'Azur. Yes, by now he had his own business jet, albeit an ageing Grumman Gulfstream III, a big American gas guzzler bought from a used plane parking lot. Another of his surefire investments which turned out to be the opposite – it cost a million dollars a year to run and was virtually obsolete before it had to be sold at little more than scrap value a few years later.

I dashed through the rain from my car to the terminal/office/reception to find just one other bloke I didn't know there waiting – about to fly off on his own somewhere I assumed. Despite both being English we eventually started making conversation.

"Where are you flying to?" I asked.

"Oh, I'm not flying anywhere," he replied. "I'm an aviation photographer and I'm waiting for this Gulfstream III to arrive. It's about the biggest plane that can safely land here, and in this weather that's going to be a challenge! Taking off again should be even more interesting – the runway's only just long enough for it. Have you seen that bank of trees at the end?"

I looked at the barricade of dark pine shielding the runway. I'm a seasoned flyer, but even still I swallowed as I told him I was due to be on that plane.

At that point Father and his crew made their noisy entrance, arriving later as they'd received a message I hadn't – namely, due to the poor visibility the plane had been delayed and was up there in the sky waiting for a window in the low cloud.

We barely had time for pleasantries before the desired window opened, and the twelve-seater poked through the gloom just a couple of hundred feet above the runway. It skidded down, and the afterburners roared as the engines went into reverse thrust to aid the skinny brakes on the slippery tarmac. The plane pitched around just a foot from the end of the runway and lurched onto the taxiway towards the terminal

Safely parked up, the pilot came into the terminal to fetch us, a waft of burnt kerosene from the afterburn following him in. I did admire the guy – both for meeting my father's extreme demands, and for doing so safely and professionally.

He took us back out to the plane through the now drizzling damp and up the rickety stairway unfurled from the fuselage. We climbed into the cramped cabin. Even in a comparatively large private jet like this there's surprisingly little room inside, and only the shortest of people can stand up straight. I bet many a WAG has been secretly disappointed if they've already experienced the spacious luxe of first class. Planes like this are also extremely noisy, with the jet engines only feet away from your ears. They fly much higher than commercial aircraft too, typically at around 44,000 feet. This gives better fuel efficiency, but it's damn cold up there, and the heating systems aren't always fit for purpose at that altitude. Especially if the plane's twenty-five years old, like this one. Having been on it just a couple of times, my wife thinks the whole jamboree is highly overrated. She'd much rather fly in a big, solid airliner.

Maybe she's right to be suspicious of private jets, the tool of choice for rendition subjects, a bird of prey ready to snatch their quarry and fly them to whatever secret bunker lies below the radar. So next time you see one push in front of you on a taxiway, remember they could as easily be heading to Guantanamo as Guadalupe.

If anybody does think flying in your own jet is actually a bit crap they're not going to admit it any time soon, and quite rightly no one's going to feel sorry for them. What you can't fail to like is the complete avoidance of any kind of check-in hassle and an extremely lax approach to security – drugs, currency, contraband, artworks – that'll do nicely, sir. Or madam.

The twelve seats on this flight are only occupied by six of us, so there is a little more space. Nearest the pilots are a seat on either side facing backwards, up against the bulkhead of the cockpit. No one is permitted in these as they face the two seats my father likes for himself and his partner Ursula, so he can have more legroom, and put his bulging and bruised briefcase in front of him. Ursula at this stage hasn't yet been assigned to the back seats and replaced with the new model. That happens not long after: twenty-seven-year-old Magda makes her first appearance at the French stud we're in the early stages of researching on this trip.

Behind are two more forward facing seats and sitting in these are a couple who are friends of my father. I say 'friends' but he and people like him, I suspect, the Bransons and Philip Greens of this world, don't have any real friends, not people they could have a natter with over a pint. The people who make up the court are either on the payroll, directly or indirectly, or along for the ride, literally in this case. Today's couple are perfectly nice people, but it's clear they're there to fill up the seats and will do exactly as asked. There's no democracy operating here.

At the back of the plane there are two three-person bench seats facing each other, and this less luxurious setting is where I'm installed opposite Ursula's nurse. Ursula's advancing Alzheimer's means she now has a constant companion, currently Andrea, a New Zealander who has decided to give over a few years of her life to the Blackburn clan for a very modest wage and a lot of travel.

Right now, there's the rather more pressing matter of getting this plane off the ground. Thank God it isn't at full operating weight. The Captain taxis back out to the end of the frighteningly short runway and turns to face the trees – are they moving up the hill to make our ascent even harder?

He then performs the aeronautical equivalent of a handbrake start – the wheels are locked, the engines scream as the throttles are set to maximum, the brakes are released and the aircraft pitches forward with the G-force of a drag racer. The runway lights flash by quicker and quicker and the plane prises itself from the ground more out of hope and fear than by science. The trees are right there, but below us, not in front, as their branches scratch at the undercarriage. Then a thump and a sharp *krackkk*.

Have we hit the woods after all? No, we've had a bird strike. A flock of crows in the pines must have been spooked, and they've flown straight up into the ascending plane. The windscreen is splintered, but luckily double-glazed, and the inner glass is intact. The pilot eases off on the power, and there's a brief conflab with air traffic control over what happens next. It's decided we can carry on, but we have to fly low and slow. Either pressurising the plane to fly at altitude or going too fast could cause the inner screen to crack, with disastrous consequences.

So our two hour trip to Nice becomes a four hour one. After the tedious crawl down, relieved by some spectacular alpine footage as we scrape the peaks, our approach is treated as a full-scale emergency. Fire trucks and ambulances are scattered around the runway like a full-size Lego disaster set. We touch down without any drama, but the response vehicles break cover anyway, following us up the runway and then escorting us to our berth. They slink away, disappointed, as the engines are switched off and whine down to a halt.

NCE

We emerge from the plane onto the concrete beach of Nice Airport. The runways stretch out into the sea on the reclaimed land, its margins bleeding into the sand. The white fuselages dazzle in the hot sun. Business jets and holiday airliners jostle for position on the apron. I breathe in the Mediterranean air, the same air which cleansed the fug of my decade of British institutional incarceration nearly forty years ago. I stayed in Cap d'Ail just along the Cote d'Azur for most of my 'gap year', though no one thought to call it that then, it was just a year off.

/

I'd left all-male Bradfield College the previous December, having failed the Oxbridge entrance exams. Or as I've been known to say, I was up at Oxford – Keble College – but only for three days. I was offered a place at the London School of Economics the following autumn. My father decided I should learn French and then work in France until my college course started.

When I travelled down, in spring '77, I didn't fly. In my car-centric family, the idea of spending time anywhere without wheels was completely alien. I drove down with my father and brother in the Mitsubishi Colt I'd been given when I passed my driving test the previous autumn. I was so nervous taking the test, especially the very first one, when my leg shook so much I managed to reverse onto the pavement, almost hitting a post box. Thank the Lord it wasn't a small child. Whatever his faults, my father could be generous, especially when something suited his grand plan. We took the backroads in the little Japanese car to save on the autoroute tolls, just stopping overnight at a random hotel in the middle of nowhere, arriving late the next evening at a campsite between Nice and St Tropez. It was owned by some friends of his, off the beaten track and nothing flash.

He stayed one night himself and then jetted off wherever.

A day or two later it was my turn to go, and I left my brother behind to help out on the campsite over Easter while I drove east for an hour to the Centre Mediterranean d'Etudes Francaises. I was to spend a month there studying, and find a job to last the rest of the summer.

At first I was homesick, but gradually life at the Centre became more interesting than life at the airport. The place was filling up for the summer with young people from all over Europe. A bunch of folk from Australia had arrived to learn French because they were heading to Montreal to open a gym. They took me in hand; I had a gang. Marty and Tony were fit and charismatic, and I reinvented myself as their cocky apprentice. Their leader, a charismatic Australian called John Valentine, was older than the rest but had a twinkle in his eye and a beautiful and steely partner, Jackie, and two equally gorgeous daughters from different earlier marriages. Both these marriages must have been to American women, because the half-sisters weren't very Aussie; Livia was dark-skinned and Latin, while blonde Tina was all Californian hippy, lots of meditating and smoking weed. I didn't have a relationship with either of them, not then, anyway, but they took me in hand as a kind of little bro. That suited me just fine.

Then Paddy and Sal arrived from Liverpool to work in the kitchens for the summer before they too went to college. At first I resented them for straying onto my patch, a jealous terrier barking them off. I know I was snotty with them. I was busy with my self-transformation, enjoying my new freedom and my friendships with all these exotic people, I didn't need some English types arriving and messing it all up, dragging me down. But... they were OK. They liked punk music. And football. And literature. I condescended to speak to them. Paddy became my best mate.

But my new flashy 19-year-old self was keeping a secret; I'd never slept with anyone. The previous summer Helen and I had snogged and fumbled for Britain, but her parents had put the kaibosh on that. Now here in France there were… possibilities. Lisa was an American straight out of school, sent to Europe for the summer to learn languages and experience the wider world. She had hair so blonde it was almost white, and big green cat's eyes. Of course I fancied her, and to my great surprise she fancied me back.

I'd stopped going to the airport to look at planes. Our French course was coming to an end. Lisa was going home to the States, I was staying put and I still hadn't found a job. On the last day. I was offered work as a caddy at the Monaco Golf Club, although it was all tips rather than a regular wage. Sitting that evening as usual in the Centre's bar and disco, I pondered taking the job. The barman, Pierre, suggested I ask about working with him behind the bar; they always needed more staff during high season. Sod carrying golf bags and working just for tips, instead I was serving espressos by day and Stellas by night. Still rubbish money, but board and lodging were thrown in – I just carried on at the Centre, swapping French lessons for bar work.

I wasn't on my own for long. I decided I was going to sleep with as many women as I possibly could, in a misguided belief that I had to make up for lost time after my late start. I'd stopped writing down plane numbers now; was I just going to start collecting girls in the same way? Every few weeks there'd be a fresh crop of students, and I was in the privileged position of bartender, meeting them all and trying out my multilingual chatlines. My stock got even higher when I was promoted to resident DJ. I'd play Donna Summer and Giorgio Moroder alongside the required Europop staples; that got them going. I must have been the only punk with a tan. I tried a few of my own records, but the students all sat down, confused. God Save the Queen? Mmm, probably.

In mid-summer I sent a letter home telling my parents what a brilliant time I was having, and explaining I thought it would be a good time to experiment with drugs. What was I thinking?! I don't know really. Whatever complaints I had about my father, my parents were generally liberal-minded and maybe I naively expected them to think this was an interesting development for their eldest son.

Instead, a letter came back by return – one of the few times my father's ever written to me (apart from the forest of faxes that would come later, when I made the terrible decision to work for him). Usually my mother dealt with all the correspondence, but this serious matter was obviously passed up the chain of command (that's how they operated) for him to deal with.

Don't do it! Or else!!

I can't remember what else he threatened, but he decided he and my mother would spend a weekend in Nice and check things out; it must have been one of the last trips they made together. They came just before the Silver Jubilee, and now I did go again to Nice airport to watch the chartered Cessna twin prop (not yet in the jet league back then) coming in over the Med.

My father must have been with Ursula for several years by that time, but you'd never have known it, and I spent a lovely weekend with my parents in and around the Hotel Negresco on the Promenade des Anglais. At some point they offered to fly me back for the Jubilee weekend so that I could celebrate with the family, the biggest national celebration since the Coronation. I accepted. With my punk inclinations I had the best of both worlds, picnicking by day and pogoing by night (what a sellout). For the Jubilee itself, we went to a medieval-style banquet on the village green and stuffed and drank ourselves stupid, but recovered enough to get to Fleet Country Club Rock Night where we made the most of the few punk tracks buried in the usual AOR crap. No More Heroes Any More. Something's Gonna Change.

Or not. When the weekend was over, I flew back to Nice, and gave my first and last interview on French radio, all about the Jubilee and the punk terror that had subverted it. Or not.

I fell back into my groove, new girlfriend every couple of weeks as the intakes changed. Liesbeth, Carola, Tania, Charlotte, Mary Beth, Gabi, Jette, another Lisa... lots more. I've thought a lot about why I behaved like that. I suppose some of it was context. We watched films like The Stud and Confessions of a Window Cleaner glamorising frequent casual sex. Sean Connery's James Bond was THE alpha male to aspire to. Certainly among male friends there was kudos in being able to 'pull'. There was my own insecurity in having been a feeble public school boy who was often the butt end of bullying. And there was the example of my own father, whom I had worshipped as well as resented. I thought I was happy living down to his womanising ways, and part of me was, for a while. But I couldn't compartmentalise like he did; emotions got in the way. I couldn't just treat women like a collector.

Part of me wished I could but I just wasn't that person, I wasn't hard enough, I wasn't selfish enough, I wasn't ruthless enough. I still feel guilty from the times I did treat women badly, and I still remember the hurt from the times women did to me what I did to them.

In the last wave of students before I went home, I properly fell in love, with Silvie the young woman from Frankfurt who was learning French before she joined Lufthansa as a flight attendant. She was nearly as tall as me, a lot better looking and funny, laugh-out-loud funny. And she loved me back.

JFK

Until the boom in charter flights taking tourists to holiday destinations in the 70s, air travel had been only for the rich. One man single-handedly kickstarted the next phase in budget travel by launching affordable scheduled flights, spawning the likes of Ryanair and Easyjet. He was Freddie Laker, who had the bright idea of creating the first 'no-frills' airline and applied for a licence for flights between London and New York at just £32.50 each way. There were to be no advance sales – people would just turn up and buy tickets on a first come, first served basis, and if you missed out, tough, you'd have to wait for the next flight. The Civil Aviation Authority eventually approved the application, against the wishes of the airline industry establishment, and finally on the 26th of September 1977 the first Laker Skytrain flew direct from Gatwick to New York for just £59 one way, less than half the standard Pan Am or TWA air fare.

The plane was one of the new wide-bodied jets, a Douglas DC-10, which later became infamous for its alleged poor safety record. The 272 passengers on the maiden flight landed safely though, as did every other passenger on a Laker DC-10 until the airline went bust in February 1982. It was a spectacular bankruptcy, one of the UK's biggest ever, with the airline owing over £250 million due to over-expansion and under-capitalisation in a difficult economic climate. Still, by then Freddie, a popular public figure, had become Sir Freddie, courtesy of the Labour Government he'd previously taken to court.

After I'd finished my first year at the LSE, the previous summer's Cap d'Ail crew were plotting how to spend the coming one. The Skytrain widened our options. Gym meister John Valentine and crew had set up in Montreal. He'd offered my new best friend Paddy and myself a job helping out at the gym; all we had to do was get there.

By July 1978 the Laker Skytrain had been running for almost a year, and while the price was still £59, the ticketing arrangements had changed. The people at Gatwick had got fed up with Laker travellers who'd missed out on a seat, hanging out and sleeping overnight at the airport waiting for the next flight. Now Victoria Station was the ticket office, the idea being that unlucky passengers could disperse into London while waiting for the next flight instead of clogging up Gatwick. The lucky ones with tickets could get the train down there.

In late June, term over, I'd driven up to Liverpool to stay with Paddy at his parents for a couple of days, stopping for a bit of planespotting on the way up, of course. My old logbook proves that I was still at it after a year at college. Apparently I saw plenty at Luton but nothing at all at Birmingham. Then we headed down to London, seeing David Bowie rocking Station to Station at Earls Court. The following Monday we were doing our own station tour of Victoria, joining the creeping Conga of an overnight queue through the terminus in the hope of getting on a flight the next day. By then British Rail must also have lost patience with all the people milling about, because there was some sort of system where you stood in line for ages and were issued with a number allowing you to leave the queue and rejoin it in the same place. Paddy and I took advantage of this to go and see Close Encounters, which with our impending adventure seemed more spectacular than it probably was. We couldn't stay in the cinema all night though, and had to spend the early hours on the stone floor of the station. It was bloody freezing, even in early July.

But it was all worthwhile, because the next morning we got our tickets, a big piece of card totally unlike the conventional paper slip in triplicate. There were still some hours before our flight, but we took the train down anyway for a change of scenery, and waited to experience no frills flying. In fact, it was pretty much like any other sort of flying, except you didn't get any catering. We knew that and had stocked up at Victoria.

I remember two things about that flight. One – an argument with Paddy about how far away another plane was. We could see another airliner flying across the Atlantic parallel to us, and Paddy asked me how far away it was. I replied that it must have been several miles away. No way, he said, it can't be more than a mile, you could barely see it if it was that far away. Despite my theorising about the average length of a runway, and how you could still see a landing plane from the other end of an airport way before it touched down, he was having none of it.

Two – well, the second thing I remember wasn't actually about the flight, but going through customs on landing. It was the standard US immigration hours-long hell, but spiced up by the fact that we were behind the American punk rocker Johnny Thunders in the queue, guitars and all. When he got to inspection, they took him to pieces, and particularly cruelly I thought at the time, smashed open his Easter eggs to check for anything inside. Afterwards, I reconsidered – it was July, so maybe they had a point.

Unlike the cattle sheds in most airports, at JFK major airlines had their own terminals, a glamorous brand statement to the travelling world. The TWA building was the apex of sixties airport design, a modernist tubular affair which looked more like a spaceship than a transportation hub, as intended. That said, smaller airlines still had to use a cattle shed, and this was where the Laker passengers got turfed out.

The same cattle shed was my only other experience of JFK: a few years earlier, our Midland Boeing 707 charter stopped off before we transferred onto our domestic flight south, our cheaper way to get to Florida. Outbound we'd just stayed in the airport between flights, but on the way back there was heavy snow, and we were delayed 24 hours. We had an unscheduled winter break in New York and enjoyed the city in a snowstorm. The whole family was put up in a downtown hotel at the airline's expense and made the most of it. We went to see Bedknobs and Broomsticks at the shabby but wonderful art deco Radio City Music Hall, shortly before its narrow escape from redevelopment as office space and subsequent rejuvenation.

Now, only a few years later though it felt like warp speed, we two student punk-wannabes were having a very different NY experience. We were getting a Greyhound bus up to Toronto to see Paddy's cousins en route to Montreal, so we had to find our way from JFK to the Port Authority bus terminal. This was way before Mayor Guiliani's 'zero tolerance' policing; this was the New York of Warriors and Last Exit to Brooklyn. With some relief we hauled ourselves onto the right bus at Port Authority. Then we noticed Paddy's guitar was missing. We'd got another bus across from the airport – it must have been left on there. Without really thinking about it, I was off the Greyhound and sprinting across to where our other bus had pulled up. The driver didn't want to let me back on, but I shrieked and gesticulated and he relented. The guitar was still there.

John Valentine was a lovely bloke and extremely generous – he'd treated me very kindly in Nice. But even then it was clear he was a something of a chancer. It wasn't a complete surprise to find the gym wasn't finished and there was no work. And we couldn't just go home because we didn't have a return ticket or the money to buy one as we'd been expecting to earn it. It became obvious there wasn't much point us both going to Montreal. Paddy could stay with his family but after a few days it became clear that I was expected to move on.

I ended up staying with Norman, a solid sort from Bridport in Dorset who'd worked with John before. It was miserable. I spent all the time on my own in his flat, nights too, while he was off at his girlfriend's. Nights were made even more lonely by the continual noise through the thin walls of a couple having sex loudly in the next apartment.

I tried half-heartedly to get a bar or restaurant job, but what work there was wasn't going to be given to a foreign punk without a work permit. Instead I half-heartedly watched aircraft on their approach to a municipal airport nearby. Plane numbers weren't really doing it for me anymore. The sense of control and completeness that I got from them had thinned to a final translucence. I gorged on Philip K. Dick and Kurt Vonnegut, making lists of those I thought might be in my *karass*, the special people in the world I had stuff in common with. And I tried to stave off depression with Vonnegut's idea that things would happen 'as they were meant to happen'.

My money and my options were running out, but unless I was in mortal danger, quite rightly any begging call home would… go begging. Then I got a call from John's stepson. He'd found some roofing work and wanted some backup.

Me? Roofer? It was work and I needed the money. After ten days we'd finished, and I got my cut, a big wodge of Canadian dollars. It was still six weeks until the start of my second year, but I had enough money now to get home, so I did.

Word was that the queues at JFK for the Skytrain were horrendous, and the NY authorities were getting heavy with potential travellers. But by now the other airlines had a response – selling 'standby' tickets. So once back in NY I went straight to the British Airways terminal and managed to get one back to Heathrow the same night, for just £88. Sneakily, the Skytrain ticket back to the UK was more expensive than the outbound fare anyway, so flying BA hardly cost me much more. And I could stuff my face and get drunk on the plane too. Which I did.

JER

Jersey's airport hugs the cliff face at the western end of the island. One minute you're flying over the choppy water and a moment later right beneath you are the rocks and scree under the lip of the runway. For years there was the wreck of an aircraft studded in the cliff-face but I think it's been removed now – not good for tourism.

I fly out every couple of years to see the firm which advises on family matters, and this time I go just a couple of weeks before the emergence of the Panama Papers, the prequel to the even more juicy Paradise Papers. The Panama edition listed a quarter of a million offshore companies set up seemingly for the purpose of global tax avoidance. If that sounds like a lot of firms, there were fifty times that number of confidential records pertaining to them. I don't know whether my father's names appeared on this list or not, and I don't really wish to. I presume not, or if he was mentioned, it was only superfluously, because there was never any response from the authorities.

Before I moved down to Somerset I'd fly from one of the London airports, but to my relief I don't have to go back up to town. There's a flight to Jersey from Exeter, less than an hour's drive away, so I can do it in a day. I set the alarm for 4.45 to catch the 7am flight, but then almost blow it by nearly running out of fuel – I hadn't filled up the car the day before and didn't take into account all the petrol stations down here are sensibly closed during uncivilised hours.

You wouldn't think a whole load of people would want to get up this early and fly from Exeter to the Channel Islands, but the plane is almost full. This airborne bus is going to both Guernsey and Jersey, the islands just a ten-minute hop apart after the not much longer flight from Exeter. My fellow passengers don't all look like bankers and tax exiles, but plenty do. A clutch of them stream off at Guernsey and a new intake streams on straight away, looking very much like the last lot with expensive leather coats and designer laptop bags. The passengers already on the plane only have to wait the few minutes the changeover takes.

I'm going out almost thirty-seven years to the day since my first visit. I can be that precise because I still have the piece of paper with the 1979 flight details – in my compulsive way, I keep every scrap. Though I don't need a bit of paper to remember it was an unusually warm spring day.

The piece of A4 (must have been one of the first, replacing foolscap) shows we left in the Colt Aviation aircraft registered G-COLT from Gloucester Staverton at 8am and went to Jersey via Southampton. Surprisingly, with my planespotter credentials, I can't remember what type of plane it was. I could probably look it up in one of my old journals. Not a jet. Some sort of twin propeller job. By then my father had stopped importing German cars (BMWs) and started to bring in Japanese ones (Mitsubishi Colts). This was an unpopular move with his conservative relatives in the armed forces, but made him even richer – hence his domicile in the Turks and Caicos Islands and advisers in Jersey. The Mitsubishi import business, the Colt Car Company, a properly registered UK company which paid its dues in corporation tax, was going so well that the company now had its own private plane, quite a rarity back in the 70s.

I'm aware I'm on dodgy ground when it comes to tax. I try and steer some sort of compromised cack-handed course which satisfies my centre-left sensibilities, but I have to admit I do, and have done, pretty well out of this state of affairs. I was sure I never wanted to be a tax exile myself, and for a long time avoided the family business altogether by working in shoe and sports retail on my own account. I've assiduously paid every penny of tax I should have and opted for UK tax status when given the option, but I've ultimately benefitted substantially from having a father domiciled overseas.

Note that people who carry out such measures refer to it as

tax avoidance rather than tax evasion. The former is supposed to be fair game while the latter is illegal, but certainly the gap between the two is becoming narrower and less distinct. And morally, is there really any difference? That's the question at the root of the revelations of the Panama and Paradise Papers.

There's no mention of all this when we meet the advisers, a week or two before the leaks. My brother has also flown in from Southampton, and my cousin-in-law from Gatwick. This triumvirate calls itself the Family Committee. We are, at least until my father manages to sack us for being 'incompetent', 'dishonest' or 'obstructive', whatever he believes at the time, in our perceived efforts to stop him doing exactly as he wishes. In my case, it's usually all three. We meet at JER and share a short taxi ride into St Helier, at the midpoint along the south shore. The capital, whose size barely justifies that title, is a discomfiting blend of tatty Victoriana and monolithic corporate indulgence in part funded by, one suspects, unpaid tax.

The advisers themselves are normal people, some of them islanders, some of them lawyers and accountants who've come over from the mainland to pursue a career. They end up maintaining and trying to protect the fortunes of very rich people against a growing regulatory framework. They probably don't even get paid all that much, not in comparison to the goldmines they're managing. There's Peter, the lawyer, a quietly spoken, gentle man in his early forties. He wouldn't be out of place as a partner at an accountant's office in a Home Counties market town. He's the person we turn to when my father decides, out of spite, he's had enough of making maintenance payments to our mother, who has no other source of income. Legality and morality don't usually align when dealing with money.

And that's the main reason I keep going with this whole charade – to ensure my mother can die in the house she's lived in for over fifty years, and help look after my wider, less fortunate family. My mother or one of my siblings being left penniless or homeless is not unrealistic.

We have our meetings with the advisers so we can plod on for another year, all that money from all those car sales gradually running out as my father blows it on yachts, private jets and young Romanian women of dubious intent. Afterwards we share a taxi back to Jersey airport where we wait for our respective flights. My brother and I swap plane nostalgia; he says he wants to come back to Jersey just to fly on one of the old Trislanders before they get taken out of service. These three-engined Trislander light aircraft, or more so their predecessor, the twin-engine Islanders, are one of the few successes of modern British aviation manufacturing. All too often British-made aircraft, like the Hawker Siddeley Trident or the Vickers VC-10, ended up being only bought by domestic airlines who were subsidised to do so by national government. But the Britten Norman Islanders found genuine international success.

They were rugged little ten-seaters which could take off and land if not on a sixpence, then on half a crown, needing only a grass or sand runway. Hence hundreds were sold all over the world, for island hopping and jungle crossing. This same brother once worked in Panama for BP (no dodgy papers then that I'm aware of, probably just dodgy dealings in oil) and we flew in one of these Islanders while I was visiting. We took off from the relatively-developed Americanised western side of the country, and crossed the Darien jungle, the still unnavigable umbilical cord between the Americas. We landed at a grass airstrip on the San Blas Islands on the east side, where indigenous Guna children ran after the plane, like streamers trailing from the wings in their bright, colourful clothes.

The plane's evolution into the larger Trislander wasn't quite such a success, but saw plenty of service in the Channel Islands, flitting from isle to isle in the full-on bright yellow and red colours of Aurigny Airlines. Weirdly, the third engine was mounted on the top of the tail plane, improbably suspended just above the heads of the passengers with only the thin skin of the fuselage in between. My brother will have to hurry if he wants to fly in one. There are still a few about, but they've been mostly replaced by the larger quieter new turboprop aircraft, like the one I'm in today.

Our reverie is brought to an end by the tannoy (actually, that's a lie – a screen flashes silently that my flight's ready for boarding) and the three of us disperse back to our Southern English destinations, Dad's Army arrows in reverse. My plane's the first of the three to leave, and it's a beautiful spring afternoon as we cross the runway threshold and climb into the clear blue air, the miracle of flight sparing us from the rocks below.

I've booked the window seat as I do whenever I can, and I enjoy the intimacy with the waves as we bounce up and down, first back to Guernsey for the ritual changeover and then on to Exeter in the setting sun. We cross the coastline near the edge of Dartmoor, the approach over the open moor and farmland so different to the congested greater London landscape I'm familiar with.

The clear air means it's decidedly chilly by the time I make the short crossing from the terminal to the car park – another welcome feature of these smaller airports. No modern 'transit system' or 'park 'n ride' bollocks. A full moon is rising; there'll be a frost. I've remembered I've got no petrol, and this being a trendy plug-in hybrid, no electricity either. It's the first Mitsubishi I've chosen and bought for myself, rather than had passed down to me. My father still gets free cars, even though he was bought out from the concession years ago. Part of the golden handshake. I ask in the terminal where the nearest petrol station is, and it's in the wrong direction but not far away – the first services on the M5 southbound.

I turn on the ignition and both gauges tell me my range is...
0 miles. I drive gingerly towards the M5, dangerously close to
tractor speed. I make it to the services, and then blast home as
quickly as I can, contemptuous of my full tank.

Not long afterwards, I read the Panama Papers reports in the
papers. A few months later, the information gets 'forgotten'. I
don't have that luxury.

HRE

In a similar vein, I don't really approve of the UK honours system. I say that from the perspective of one whose parents both received an OBE. People say you can buy an honour, a knighthood even; you can certainly buy an OBE. My father did, as far as I could see.

In the 70s my father was a major contributor to the Liberal party. My grandfather stood for parliament for the Liberals, as did my father, as did I – well, the Liberal Democrats by the time I stood – all of us unsuccessfully, par for the Liberals' course it has to be said. But my father was a major party donor, and that's why he got his honour. I recall the Liberal leader Jeremy Thorpe and his wife Marion coming for Sunday lunch a few times. I don't remember it very well, because he was one of those people who didn't attempt to connect with children and young teenagers – not us, anyway. But he was kind enough, and seemed gentle and cheerful. The dog killing incident happened during this period, and it was very difficult to imagine Jeremy issuing death threats.

I don't know whether they came to lunch for social reasons or because he was cultivating my father – probably a bit of both. And I don't remember how much my father gave the Party, but it was into six figures, I'm fairly sure. Whatever the amount, it was sufficient to swing the OBE. Later on my father also gave big sums of money to London Zoo, indeed helped them survive by underwriting them through a sticky patch in the early 90s. To his lasting frustration though, he was never granted a knighthood, despite the best efforts of the Zoo people. I was even given the job of nagging those responsible at the Zoo to exert more pressure and find out why he hadn't been given it! I think it was partly due to his tax affairs. But if it had only been that, maybe they would have still knighted him, they do plenty of other tax exiles after all. But by that time the Romanian ex-prostitute in her twenties was his steady companion, even on official visits to the Zoo; they all found it a bit too embarrassing.

My mother worked harder for her OBE, gaining it in the 1990s for services to the British Red Cross. It does have to be said she was able to devote her time because she was wealthy enough not to work and could afford full-time childcare. She had taught biology at the local girls High School, but when this came to an end she started volunteering. She became president of the Red Cross county division and thus received her honour, but had worked her way up from the local branch, utilising her considerable management, personnel and fundraising skills along the way. So she was no mere figurehead.

In this capacity, she was invited to visit the Mbabane Red Cross set-up in Swaziland, now Eswatini, which was twinned with her county, Berkshire. It was the time of a refugee crisis in neighbouring Mozambique, and significant aid efforts were being launched from the UK via Mbabane. She invited my father to accompany her, but he declined – poverty-stricken African countries were hardly his choice destination, and anyway he was spending more time with Ursula.

My mother then asked me. So one summer morning in the early 80s I was with her at Heathrow Terminal 3 waiting for a flight to Johannesburg. There wasn't anything remarkable about that leg of our journey, from what I remember it was an overnight flight landing at Jo'burg the next morning. I do recall there was a six-hour lay-off there before the connecting transfer to Manzini, the Swazi airport, and we weren't allowed to leave the terminal.

Eventually our flight was called, and we walked across the tarmac in the hot afternoon sun to a bright blue Fokker F28. Meet the Fokkers. The Dutch-built F27 was a versatile twin-piston workhorse doing service all over the world, and the newer F28 jet engine version fulfilled a similar role. If Concorde is a sleek racing car, the Fokkers are stubby little rally numbers that twist and scrabble through the frequent thermals and choppy turbulence of the African skies. The pilots chivvy them along, employing handbrake turns over the hills and jungles to avoid the peaks and find the best approaches.

As you might imagine our one hour-something flight to the small kingdom of Swaziland really felt like flying – not one of those European commutes where you take off, fly in a straight line for however long, and then land again. We pitched and pivoted, all the while watching the setting sun and the shadows lengthening over the moss green jungle and red ochre earth below. Then with a final pirouette, we tumbled down to the short runway of Manzini and began our week in Swaziland.

We escaped finally from the chaotic arrivals lounge populated with rather too many overly relaxed gun-toting policemen for my liking. We located our battered Toyota hire car and found our way to our modest hotel, the Lugoso Sun, on the short road from Manzini to Mbabane, the capital.

That was our base for the week, alternating days spent on Red Cross duty with leisure time trying to spot the sparse wildlife. We visited various clinics and outposts, but the most enduring memory was our trip to a refugee camp on the border with Mozambique. Definitely not my father's idea of a family holiday. That said, all the children had enough to eat; enough to keep starvation at bay anyway, and had some sort of clothing. And could smile and laugh at the strange white people.

I clicked with Constance, the young woman who ran the Mbabane Red Cross, not in any romantic manner but in a professional sort of way. The harsh realities of the situation forced a degree of maturity on me, and when she related how she hadn't seen her husband for months and wasn't entirely sure where he was, it made my post-adolescent relationship issues seem as trivial as they were. He had left the country and gone into hiding, fearing for his life as a perceived enemy of the South African security forces.

I enjoyed reprising the support role to my mother, one I'd played since I was very young, when my father disappeared on his endless business trips. My mother worried every time he was late home, doing God knows what – he didn't deserve to be worried about. My mother had little enthusiasm for food at the best of times and pecked at her food. She never had an evening meal at home so we didn't either, lunch being the main event, then bread, butter, biscuits and cake at five o'clock with a bowl of cereal before bed. Now in the hotel I could and did have dinner, and she looked on – her nervousness about food exponentially increased by the African menu. Then we'd read, talk and play Scrabble during the rapidly-dark evenings until it was time for bed.

On one excursion to a barren game park we got caught out by this sudden nightfall, and had to drive the clunky Toyota along the dodgy roads back to the hotel in total darkness. Finding myself tailgated by a big Jeep whose driver obviously knew the terrain, I pulled over briefly into what looked like a crawler lane, but it was merely a few random yards of hard shoulder and I was suddenly navigating off-road. I managed to get back onto the tarmac but the Toyota had definitely become even clunkier. Whatever, it seemed to still work.

The car lasted out the week, and though I was terrified that they'd find out it was badly broken underneath when we returned it at Manzini airport, no one said a word, and there were no hits on my credit card some time later. Just bad luck on the poor sod who hired it after me.

We took off again in another little Fokker twin jet, leaving the grilled Swazi earth behind. You may have noticed that while this chapter has featured the customary dollop of plane action it's called HRE for Harare Airport, and there's been no mention of it yet. Well, I don't know why the routing was as such, but although we flew into Manzini via Johannesburg we flew back

124

home via Harare. Again, there was a lag between our connecting flights, but the hours spent in Harare were very different to those passed in the confines of Jo'burg Airport.

We got to Harare late afternoon, and here we were allowed to leave the terminal. We found a taxi and negotiated an acceptable rate to spend the next few hours touring the capital. A good plan turned into a great one; Chuma, our driver, was friendly and had a wealth of knowledge about his home city. We put ourselves in his capable hands, although I'm ashamed to admit I can't remember much about our tour. What I do remember is that at the end we still had some time to spare before our flight, so Chuma took us to a café/bar he knew. We weren't disappointed – the simple little hut was a very hospitable family-run place. Of course my mother declined to eat anything and just had a bottle of Coca Cola (no ice), but I enjoyed my fried chicken washed down with a cold beer.

All a whole lot better than sitting in another terminal for hours on end, but of course that's where we ended up. We sat by the window looking across to the enormous BA 747 being fuelled and loaded under the floodlights, its primary colours jagged against the earth tones of the African dusk. As it grew darker whole constellations of moths and insects emerged from the heavens, radiated by the artificial light, filling the view from our plate glass window. Eventually the flight was called; no walkways or airbridges here, just a long walk across the tarmac in the steamy night air, our own Casablanca moment, real travellers ready to cross continents. Then hundreds of passengers clanking up metal staircases front and rear, filling the cool empty shell with their warm bodies.

Finally, everyone on board, the doors are locked and the light dimmed. It takes an eternity to taxi to the end of the runway, seemingly miles from the terminal. We turn around, halt for a moment; the pilot winds up the engines to full throttle. HRE is one of the highest international airports in the world, at 1483 metres higher than any point in Britain. Every ounce of power in the Rolls Royce turbines will be needed to get this fully-laden beast into the thin air and up through it. All four engines screaming, the brakes are released, and with a jerk the Jumbo moves tentatively along the runway. Slowly, surely too slowly, the velocity increases. I knew this would be one of the longest take-offs I'd ever experienced, so I'm timing it – a minute has passed, and we're still only making modest progress along the runway, no suggestion yet that the wheels can peel themselves from the earth. But then, after a whole two minutes, the nose slowly begins to rise, and the rest of the plane grudgingly follows into the darkness, bidding a reluctant farewell to Africa.

DOL

Fast forward to the Sport of Kings.

My father had moved his horseracing operation from Spain to France, but not to the Cote d'Azur – he chose (or his trainer persuaded him to choose in a rare case of external influence) Normandy. As the French-speaking son, it became part of my turf, excuse the pun. I was responsible for the overall running of the place, which I did for the next four years. As such, I went over to the stables just outside Pont l'Eveque nearly every month. Driving via the Eurotunnel or by train via the Eurostar to Paris both took six or seven hours, so the quickest way was to fly into nearby Deauville-Saint-Gatien, DOL.

The challenge with Deauville was finding flights from the UK into the small airport. When we were in the throes of making the purchase (I'd call it due diligence, but that would be flattering unto our cause) there was a tiny airline which had a scheduled service there from Shoreham Airport near Brighton. SkySouth flew an eight-seater Piper Navajo several days a week (I think that's the only plane they flew). Often my wife or a business colleague came with me, but regularly we were the only passengers on the plane. Surely not economic to operate?

After several scouting visits and preliminary discussions we ended up successfully buying the stud from its German seller, part of a major publishing family, at a knockdown price – he had bought it for his horse-loving wife but was now going through a divorce and wanted out quickly. Having completed the deal at a hotel just outside Deauville, we set off for the airport for the journey home in deteriorating weather and high winds. The three of us – me, my wife, my colleague – were the only ones in the terminal. There are very few scheduled flights heading anywhere from Deauville but it can feel very busy in the small building if there's a charter flight (or two!) going somewhere hotter. This wasn't one of those days.

Scheduled departure time approached and there was no sign

of the plane. Then a man in glasses appeared from nowhere and accosted us. "It's too windy for the plane to land here, so it's gone to Le Havre instead and we're arranging for a taxi to take you there." Being right on the coast, you wouldn't expect Le Havre to be any less pummelled, but Deauville's airport, despite being a couple of miles inland, is built high on a plateau.

With little choice in the matter, the taxi arrived and we piled in for the half-hour drive over the Pont de Normandie to Le Havre. By now proper maritime winter weather had taken hold, and we got a good lashing making our way across the tarmac to the too-small Piper shivering in the wind. We took off into the grumpy late afternoon sky and the plane launched into a game of pinball with the buffeting clouds. In a strange way, I prefer turbulence in a small plane to experiencing it in an airliner; I'd rather be right there with the pilots, seeing them do their job and looking calm and in control. I can't say the same for my colleague Nigel, who was clearly terrified. I have to say, it was pretty bad, certainly among the worst I've known. My wife can be a poor traveller, but on this occasion I think the romance and excitement of the journey touched her. There *was* romance in it; the punishing weather accelerated nightfall and we evoked the primitive flying of de Saint-Exupéry, spotting the navigational lights of the ships below in the fleeting gaps through the clouds.

And then, the weather cleared a fraction, and the coastal lights of Sussex shone their welcome through the murk. Shortly afterwards, their horizontal line was slashed by the perpendicular of Shoreham's runway lighting, a beacon to aim for as the little plane took its knocks and sideswipes. We landed without incident, but that was our last flight on SkySouth. Not because the experience had put us off but because, as feared, the airline went into administration. I do wonder if that diverted last flight and our expensive taxi journey was the final nail in the cabin.

When my father came to visit he arrived in his own jet. Of

course. One time there was a more of a hubbub at the stables in anticipation of his arrival than usual: he was bringing a new girlfriend. He wouldn't sleep in the main building, a beautiful Norman 15th century manor house, but in a little cottage across the road for the sake of his privacy. Although I had the misfortune to be there for his visit, I didn't see him or the new girlfriend when they arrived that evening and went straight over the road (I had the dubious pleasure of being told by a jockey who was on the plane that she was undoubtedly a prostitute). His assessment was correct – Magda was the Romanian chancer who'd snared my father in Malaga and cashed in. That said, he was quite happy to be snared. Luckily for the rest of us, Magda didn't appreciate horses or Normandy whose weather was far too British for her liking, so we saw very little of her.

However, our refusal to welcome her into the family and our inability to refrain from trying to tell him what she really was and what she wanted from him drove a further wedge between us. He should have listened; she did of course later decide to cash in. Surprise, surprise – the million Euro ski lodge they'd supposedly bought together turned out to be in her name, and legal attempts to recover it when she vanished were fruitless. I received no thanks for having been proved right – if anything, it ramped up the level of resentful bitterness.

SkySouth having flown into the ether, and private jets being beyond my pay grade, I started flying over to Deauville in an even smaller plane. The stables in France had been used by the German family as a stud farm, but my father's intention was to train horses there rather than breed them, so some changes had to be made – a gallop had to be installed across some of the fields so they could have a good run out. Specialist help was needed with this, and the person we found just happened to be based next to a farmer who just happened to have his own plane which just happened to be kept in a field right next to Thruxton Airport (more an airfield in the middle of a racetrack really) in Hampshire.

Mark, the farmer, with extraordinary generosity was prepared to fly us out to Deauville for no charge except for the landing fees. Though I offered, he didn't even want money for the fuel, let alone his time. His logic was that he needed to do a certain number of flying hours each year to keep his licence current, so he might as well be flying to France as anywhere else.

This was modern flying at its most basic level. We'd only go if the conditions were fine and visibility good. We'd clamber in over the wing and through the tiny door of the single engine Robin aircraft, me in the front next to the pilot claiming beanpole rights, and the equine expert in the cramped back seat. Because the field we took off from was parallel with the Thruxton runway across the A303, Mark could use the control tower there for take-off clearance. Once the little plane got above the hedge rows, we could see the other aircraft to our left as we climbed out to the right, heading for the south coast.

Compared with the larger planes, it was slow going, the speedo of the Robin barely troubling triple digits, but the experience was more immersive, more engaging. Tracking all the instruments aligned in front of me, scanning the sea and sky through the expanses of unpressurised glass. Eventually the French coast crept into existence at the fuzzy margin of the horizon, and the port and familiar runway of Le Havre would take form. We'd pass over the mouth of the Seine and the airport of Deauville was there in front of us, perched on the head of the plateau, surrounded by its fringe of forest away from the shore behind the town. We'd take the long way round, heading inland before turning back out to sea to land into the prevailing offshore wind.

With no shuttle buses to wait for or baggage to reclaim, we'd walk straight through the nominal customs hall and be with our waiting driver within minutes of touchdown. This waiting driver was almost always Graham, a long-time employee of my father's who'd come out of semi-retirement in Nice to run the stable on a daily basis – not the horse racing aspects, but the day-to-day estate management.

For a couple of years, this arrangement seemed to work well, all in all, but as so often happens there was a falling out. This falling out was between my father and the trainer. It was inevitable – and not just with hindsight, I'd warned the trainer it would happen. He always knows best, my father, even when he doesn't, so the trainer had to go. The numbers weren't stacking up: more and more horses, none being sold, so higher and higher costs with only a limited income from winnings. Romanian Magda preferred to go to hot places, another factor. It became my job to sell the stables again.

By now, CityJet, at the time a subsidiary of Air France/KLM operating some of their commuter routes, had inaugurated a direct service from London City Airport to Deauville, and this was perfect for me – a quick tube/DLR journey right to the terminal. This was just as well, as I now found myself going over to France more weekly than monthly.

We'd invited a trio of property agents to value the place, and they all came to the similar conclusion of a figure healthily in excess of our purchase price. Father, however, indicated he wanted to secure a figure twice as high again. While we were still musing on this, one of the agents, a Franco-Dutch woman who'd charmed and been charmed by Graham, approached us to say that a major overseas racing dynasty was interested in the stables.

In the circumstances, I decided to offer it at the price my father wanted. That is, at twice the valuation. To our amazement they said yes. Now we had to get the deal done.

That was a challenge. The first complication was establishing just who we were dealing with. The dynasty which was purchasing seemed to have many offshoots; which exactly was the buyer? Who was speaking for them? All these tributaries had various representatives who claimed to be acting on their behalf, all wanting a slice of the cake. You bake a cake that large, you find an awful lot of people want their piece of it. Eventually we established who the principals, and their legitimate representatives, were. Now we could get on with the actual transaction.

Or could we? Not unless we had the approval of a government agency called SAFER, apparently. SAFER is the Société d'Aménagement Foncier et d'Établissement Rural, and has the right of first purchase of most rural property coming onto the market in France. In theory they could have blocked our deal, claiming they wanted our land. However, like so many other 'interested parties', they didn't actually want our land, what they wanted was their slice of the gateau. This meant some complicated arrangement whereby we would sell it to SAFER, but almost simultaneously they would sell it on to the racing dynasty. The advantage for SAFER was that while we were subject to some sort of sales tax, they were exempt, so when they moved it on they could pocket the difference. There was no disadvantage to us, apart from the stress of having another layer of complexity and the personal stress on me and my involuntary French language refresher course, specialising in agricultural vocab.

We were almost there. Then Graham, the person also responsible for the company signatures, fell seriously ill with stomach problems. The day before the deal was to be completed in Paris, I had to get his signature on all the papers. I made the usual trip to Normandy and borrowed a car from the stable garages, a Lancia Delta integrale bought for investment purposes, no Graham to pick me up this time, obviously. It was evening visiting time at the forbidding multi-storey Lisieux hospital, a building dwarfing all the others in the modest market town. Graham had just come out of surgery, but had apparently come round and was able to see me. It felt like a 'Scruples' question: you desperately need to do a business deal, but to do so you need to obtain the signature of a man who's lying seriously ill in hospital stuffed full of tubes – what do you do?

Well, now I know my answer. I found Graham on the umpteenth floor, and did my best to show my genuine concern and establish whether he was comfortable with signing the papers. He took it all extremely well; he understood the situation and he was willing to sign. I produced my clipboard and put pen and papers in front of him.

Once I had the signatures, I stayed with him for as long a time as we both found comfortable, and then I descended back to the car park and the Lancia rally car. Then back to the Haras for a few hours' sleep before the morning train journey to Paris for the signing.

The conference room at the lawyers' offices was brim full with mediocre men in ties, and a formidable French woman heading up the buying delegation. The two suits from SAFER were there to enjoy their momentary ownership of the stud. After all the shenanigans of the transaction the actual completion went smoothly, and by lunchtime I was out on a Parisian boulevard in the damp autumn mist. I was very satisfied, somewhat relieved but also sad that I would never again look across from the terrace of the beautiful Haras at sunset through the tall trees beyond the horses, wine glass in hand.

I got a grip on myself and rang my father to tell him the deal had been done. "For the full amount?" he asked.

"Yes."

"Seriously?"

"Yes."

He was pleased. Very pleased. He actually told me that this made up for all the money I'd lost! That was soon forgotten, but I enjoyed the moment.

I took the Eurostar back to London. No point in flying. And shortly after this, CityJet flights from LCY to Deauville ceased anyway. The airline lost over €50m in a year and Air France got shot of it. It's still going, now under Irish ownership, but it seems to a falling number of destinations. Whatever, I wish them well, they looked after me.

Happy times.

LCY

Not long after my regular flights from LCY to Deauville, I'm in London and find I've a few hours to kill before I have to catch the train home to Somerset, following our self-exile. My business in town is done with, but I can't get an earlier service as I've got an advance £10 sooper-dooper saver. So I decide to do something I haven't done before with this, and visit an airport just for the hell of it. No planes will be taking off in the making of this chapter. Not with me on board, anyway.

I check out the possibility on my phone – it will take forty minutes to get to London City Airport from where I am in Holborn. And then just twenty-three to get back to Waterloo. It's doable. That's one of the reasons it's my favourite airport, so accessible. When we lived in London, I'd get the Jubilee Line and then merely had to change platforms at Canning Town before coming right into the middle of the airport a few stops later – no long-term car park or shuttle bus nonsense.

Although I won't be flying there today, it's not as if I haven't been a frequent flyer from LCY. There was that purple patch during the years of going to Cork when the short-lived Jet Magic flew their half-empty Embraers out of City. Then there were the City Jet twin-props hopping across the channel to Deauville. Shame it all stopped, I used to love those flights. The pilot snatching the plane up before it tipped off the short runway besieged by the docklands inlets. The sharp ascent over the city, the wheels scraping the spires of Canary Wharf. Then wheeling the Dome for a panoramic swooping survey of the capital before shooting off down the Thames. Clipping off the shingly corner of Kent and then over water all the way to Le Havre and the descent to the Deauville plateau.

Now it's a climate-change hot stuffy sort of an afternoon as I get on the tube at Chancery Lane to go and not fly from LCY. London is doing an imitation of a Mediterranean city as dishabillé office workers sip iced lattes at pavement cafes. I go just two stops to Bank and follow the subterranean maze to the Docklands Light Railway. I'm struck by the contrast to the Victorian scruffiness of the Central Line.

Then we pass the lowly concrete shed of Billingsgate Market, transposed here from its riverside berth in the 80s when water frontage became valuable real estate. You wonder if the smell of fish gets up the sneering noses of the overlooking neoliberal edifices – Bank of America, J.P. Morgan, HSBC – but no doubt their air conditioning sanitises it.

It's not just the buildings outside which tell a tale of two cities. Inside the carriage, although intermingled, the passengers form two distinct groups. The people with luggage and the people without; the people who get off at LCY, and those who carry on and go under the river – to King George V, a posh name for North Woolwich, and Woolwich Arsenal itself. The indigenous Londoners look down, read the Metro freesheet and listen to music through their earphones. Meanwhile the noisy excited travellers in their shorts and shades huddle round their luggage and excitedly look out for landmarks over the post-industrial scenery.

I arrive at the airport and walk the short distance to the terminal – one building fuses into the other. I touch in with my Oyster travelcard, avoiding the trap that I cynically suspect Transport for London of setting; there's no barrier to go through, so it wouldn't surprise me if thousands of unseasoned travellers inadvertently pass through without paying, and then get rumbled by the ticket inspectors on the train. How many exactly, I wonder? That would be worth a Freedom of Information request.

I've got an hour and something to kill before I have to get the train to Waterloo, so I go and get myself a coffee at Pret a Manger, thinking I'll make a start on writing some notes. I much prefer Pret to Starbucks, which I've never been able to forgive for gazumping me when I tried to buy a shop in North London.

Starbucks used the money from the taxes they were avoiding to pay a £50,000 premium which I could never match. I'm sure Pret would be pleased to know I've also forgiven them for the unfortunate period when McDonalds was a major stakeholder. Plus the coffee's better, in my humble opinion.

I often wonder how close I might have been to bumping into my father at an airport. There must have been times we'd come close in Munich, me there twice a year for trade shows and him with his car stuff and German girlfriend and apartment. But in fact it was my wife who did finally encounter him, here at LCY. On the rarest of occasions she was flying somewhere without me, to Copenhagen to help look after the child of a very sick friend for a few days. I can't remember where my father was coming from or going to, just passing through, we didn't even know he was in the country. They put on a good show of being pleased to chance upon each other and were civilised.

I thought about the time my wife and I had deliberately met him at an airport. One Christmas he couldn't even manage to give us an evening slot at his golf club or a local hotel, so we were given the opportunity to meet him at Heathrow as he passed through from warmer climes on his way to yuletide in Ireland. We found him and Ursula on a bench in the arrivals hall, surrounded by a landfill of plastic bags in varying states of decay, the way he always travelled. Hermes? Nein danke. We had a quick drink and then the routine one-way transfer of information (instructions) and then got the tube back into London. Merry Christmas everybody.

That set me off on a reverie I often indulge in – a kind of Sliding Doors of near misses. How often do we almost cross paths with someone we might have known? Even be in the same airport at the same time as someone we've loved? I fantasise about all the people I've valued being fitted with a tracker. These trackers would cause orange lights to flash showing their location on an enormous world map in a 70s Bond film type subterranean control room. I'd have a tracker too, with a green light, and when my light synced with one of the red ones, someone in the control room would alert me, "DCB at fifty metres! Repeat, DCB at fifty metres!"

My wife, who tends to know these things, tells me there's already an app for this.

I thud back to reality – armed policemen at just ten metres, armed policemen at ten metres. Right across from my perch in Pret, there are two guys with all the gear, including machineguns slung casually over their shoulders. They're the type who would have spotted the younger, punkier me from way back and ushered me into one of those side rooms.

"What exactly are you doing here, if you're not travelling anywhere?"

"Well, I'm doing some research on this book I'm writing…" Long pause.

"You'd better come with us…"

But now I'm just a middle-aged bloke with greying hair, I'm as invisible to them as I am to all the people half my age jetting off somewhere exciting. It intrigues me which people end up being the ones empowered to brandish deadly weapons with complete legitimacy. These two are entirely different to each other; one looks like any old bloke you'd see down the pub – mid-forties, balding, bit of a paunch, and the other looks like he could be on a transfer from an Eastern European secret police section. Really Slavic looking, hard and sharp, he could kill just with his cheekbones. They get bored with surveying my patch, and wander off to patrol another corner of the compact terminal.

While police here may be indifferent, I've found the UK Border Agency to be offensive, bureaucratic and pompous. It's like that pretty much wherever you come across it. For a small airport there can be big queues of people trying to get through

Passport Control at peak times. What really winds me up though is the rudeness of it all. No 'Welcome to Britain' or anything like that, just petty signs about getting your passport ready, not even the word 'please'. So much for British manners. Maybe I'm just sick of power plays.

I finish my coffee and my notes and begin to head off, thinking I might take a few photographs on my way. I go outside the building, but it's like one of those US-inspired transport hubs where there's no obvious route for pedestrians. Maybe the DLR station itself would be a better vantage point given it's open to the elements at one end, and I should be able to see the planes approaching over the City. I check the train times on the electronic display – I can get one in ten minutes and still comfortably get to Waterloo on time. I walk all the way to the end of the platform (having touched in my Oystercard, of course) and I'm waiting for my plane. A train comes and goes – I'm the only one who doesn't get on it. Still no planes. Then I see the two police from the terminal approaching. There's no one else, they must be heading for me. Just as I'm rehearsing my lines, they suddenly disappear down a staircase between us which I hadn't even noticed. It's almost an anti-climax. Even when I'm obviously watching the planes and not bothering to get on a train, they don't want to know. I really am the invisible man.

Finally a plane approaches and I snap away on my phone, an Alitalia Embraer 190 twin jet. Then my DLR arrives and I get on, looking at the images on my phone. Mmm, not promising. Is it a bird? Is it a plane? Later when I look at them on my laptop they're not much better. I do have one LCY picture I want to use, from a few years back. Sitting on a plane, ready to depart I looked back towards the City and could see a plume of smoke coming out of the main Canary Wharf tower. I tweeted a photograph, more in curiosity than alarm, and was quickly informed that was normal, the emission from the air con system. I could use that pic, I think, but the rest... So I asked the nice people at LCY, and they sent me some proper pictures. My favourite airport.

So what will become of City Airport when Brexit's happened and all the banks have moved abroad? Will the City skyscrapers morph into Bladerunner tower blocks, a High-Rise housing solution for our island state? Maybe LCY never really belonged in London after all, and a big ship will come up the Thames estuary and tow it out across the sea to Copenhagen or Amsterdam while the rest of the world carries on without us.

LXX

It's a very long time since I got the binoculars out and spotted a plane, but I still dream about them. Often. Not quite a recurring nightmare, but a recurring theme – planes crashing.

Usually I'm back at my mother's house, which I left forty years ago, when I first started looking up at them in the sky. Even the earliest dream I can remember was about planes – sort of. I imagined I was awake and outside very early on a summer morning, hours before anyone was up but still light. I saw something overhead which looked like a hovercraft. Then I found out hovercraft couldn't fly thousands of feet up. That didn't dampen my conviction in what I'd seen; I didn't believe it was a dream, though it must have been. And I had to admit, I did have a track record. I was a sickly child and often in a high fever, to the point where I'd hallucinate. First there was the monkey under my bed, then (don't laugh) Tich and Quackers living behind the headboard. Tich and Quackers were Ray Allen the TV ventriloquist and his dummy, so in all probability they weren't living behind my headboard. But for quite a while I was very scared about going to bed.

I'm less confused now. When I have a dream, I know it's a dream. My last plane crash nightmare was very vivid. There was a four-engined British Airways jet – not a real aircraft, some amalgamation of an Airbus and a jumbo, and it was pointing down at an improbable angle, and far too low. That's a common pattern in the dreams; the planes are always wrong – wrong altitude, wrong attitude. I've watched thousands of planes from the roof terrace at my mother's, and in an easterly wind they all approach Heathrow the same way. In a westerly wind they take off over the house and are too high to catch by the time they pass over the house. Landing, they make a gentle loop onto finals, then the slide down across Windsor Great Park and over the castle. But these dream planes have gone rogue.

The last dreamliner was just a few hundred meters from the

house, far too close to the fields behind, pointed towards the earth. Sure enough it went down, the point of impact hidden behind a dreamed-up tower block, part of the expanding new town nearby. True, the town is in reality spreading across the Green Belt, but at a fraction of the rate it does in my dreams. There was a moment's peace before the fireball and smoke erupted over the building, and the boom shook its windows.

The nightmare landscape around my mother's house must be littered with the broken fuselages from all these dreams. This time was worse than usual; I was out in the open, but there was no time to make a futile run towards the plane before the block of flats tumbled down, over the house. My mother miraculously survived, but soon the security services (I was glad to see they were still functioning in this post-apocalyptic netherworld) had walled off her home. Despite their efforts, I could see through a gap to people looting the rooms, shredding the tissue of my heritage.

Like the broken planes of my dreams, LXX Lincoln International Airport doesn't really exist. I made up the IATA code, which doesn't relate to any real airfield, and Lincoln is the name given to the fictional *Airport* in Arthur Hailey's novel, the first disaster blockbuster. The novel reflected the glamour of modern air travel, but also the terror of it; why wouldn't one of these metal tubes just fall out of the sky, especially on a stormy, snowy night? My own nightmares illustrate these deep fears we have about planes and flying; even me, someone who loves the bloody things and loves flying in them and has done so hundreds of times. Why are we so scared?

Planes do crash, of course. There's a piece of 'raw data' I still have, a list of spotted plane numbers written on the blank pages of an unused old diary. I would say from the traffic recorded they were the haul from a day's work at Heathrow. There's twenty-two numbers on the left-hand page; I did some research on these, and I can see at least two of them have crashed.

Still, as they're always telling you, air travel is one of the safest modes of travel. It's true if you measure it in terms of fatalities per kilometre travelled; 0.05 deaths per billion on a plane compared with 3.1 per billion on a car. Which is why an awful lot of planes fly for thirty or forty years and don't crash. So what happens to them? Well, they end up in a graveyard. Or a boneyard, as they call them in aviation circles. We visited one once when we were on one of our US holidays, Mojave Air and Space Port. A trip to Disneyland which we subverted to our plane habit, Jumbo not Dumbo. Rows and rows of airplane husks neatly lined up in the desert, aircraft bones never rotting in the hot sun.

The largest boneyard is at Davis Monthan Airbase in Arizona (which incidentally boasts a high incidence of UFO sightings, but let's stick with planes emanating from Planet Earth), and this houses over 4,000 wrecks, although admittedly most of those are military aircraft rather than airliners. The one we visited, Mojave, is home to a thousand airliners, and between them the aircraft graveyards of the West Coast States house tens of thousands of planes.

So if air travel's so safe, and all these planes end up in the desert after flying for decades without ever crashing, why do people get so scared?

There is of course the terrorist incident that can never be ignored or forgotten. The images of the airliners puncturing the Twin Towers are seared on everyone's consciousness, images so extreme that they contort into nightmares at the very edge of credibility, exaggerating our fear of flying and ever ready to flare up in our imagination. I do wonder if my own horrible plane dreams would have been so frequent and so vivid if September 11th 2001 had never happened. Thank God my visions are just dreams, and no one I know was on those planes or in those buildings.

But like everyone else I won't forget my first exposure to those judderingly graphic film clips, at the beginning of the forty-eight hours when we wondered if civilisation had ended; if Bush would push the button deep underground in the remote bunker he himself had been renditioned to at Offutt Air Force base, Nebraska. I was working up in Northumberland running another shoe retail business, that day making store visits with the Property Manager. Having heard the news, the staff in the Swalwell branch on the Newcastle outskirts had turned the shop TV on. We watched as stunned as everyone else while the unimaginable happened on the screen in front of us, numb with anticipation at what might happen next. The phone lines creaked and mobile networks fragmented as folk failed to give and receive token reassurance to and from loved ones. I eventually got through to my wife, hundreds of miles south.

I was due to fly the very next day and I did, from Newcastle to Dusseldorf for a trade fair. There were a few of us going – I was boss, but the whole buying team were on the trip. I gave people the choice about coming, and everyone did. I have never known a terminal as quiet. Barring the odd stab at gallows humour, passengers shuffled through passport control and an unsurprisingly rigorous luggage check with barely a murmur, the usual airport hubbub switched off.

Nothing happened, of course. And the truth is, it very seldom does – since 9/11, the American translation we've been forced to adopt, not a single British life has been lost in a terrorist attack on aviation. But the attack is still used an excuse for the ever more elaborate and time-consuming processes of airport security.

As someone who's spent too many hours of his life in those secret little rooms just off corridors through customs halls, I'm well aware of the inconsistencies. Often when I was working in France I'd drive rather than fly, especially if I had to take a load of stuff with me. Frequently I'd be waved through security without a glance. One time, just as I reached the UK barrier on my way out, I couldn't find my passport anywhere, and pulled up to one side while I looked for it. The officials wandered up to me, and I braced myself for their questions. They just asked me what was wrong, and when I explained they merely waved me through, telling me the French side didn't normally bother to check documents. Sure enough, they didn't, and I carried on my way.

The only time I've ever been in real danger in the air was when my own father was the pilot – the helicopter trip home from school. But when I was that schoolboy, I found planes reassuring; the tail lights of that evening jumbo might be Daddy coming home. Now I dream of jumbo jets crashing into the fields around the old family house. We wonder how long my mother can stay there before the money runs out. The family's gone from rags to riches and almost back again, not in three generations but in just one. My father has blown all the money on women, boats and yes, private jets, and is seemingly determined to live long enough to finish the job despite kicking death's door more than once. I still have desires, ambitions and dreams, but I wonder if I have the energy and the years left to fulfil them. That's the real nightmare.

SYD

My mother mentioned she'd had a flyer in the post: Heathrow was celebrating its 70th birthday by inviting local residents to send in stories of their experience of the airport (yes, she still lives there, in that same house on the flightpath, the place we made our bus trips to LHR from forty odd years ago). She asked me if I'd type up something she'd handwritten and submit it for her online, a competition requirement that was beyond her. Well, she is well into her eighties. I agreed, and said I'd pick up the piece next time I visited. A few weeks later, we had a family get together (supposedly a summer barbeque but torrential rain snuffed that out) and I took the item home with me afterwards.

I checked out the website that evening and discovered the very next day was the closing date. Maybe I could enter something I'd written as well. I looked at the criteria – one of which was *How the story shows personal progression/development as a result of your Heathrow experience*. I supposed my Heathrow chapter fitted, or part of it at least, at a push. I had a busy few hours. First I typed up my mother's story and entered that. It was an interesting account of how her own flight had been diverted to Entebbe after a Lufthansa 707 had crashed at Nairobi in the 70s. My parents' intended safari instead began with involuntary hospitality courtesy of one Idi Amin. He detained all the passengers and used the opportunity to give them 24 hours of Ugandan cultural indoctrination. In her piece, my mother made a powerful case that this may have been a dress rehearsal for the seizure of the El Al plane there a while later, an incident immortalised by the successful rescue of the passengers and its subsequent film dramatization, Victory at Entebbe.

My own tale of planespotting at Heathrow would be more pedestrian, but I set to work on my LHR chapter, cutting the two thousand plus words down to the five hundred necessary for the competition, chucking some of the more personal baggage out of the hold. Late that night and minutes before the deadline, finally happy with my edit, I emailed my entry too, and promptly forgot all about it.

A couple of weeks later I got an email, headed *Special Delivery, Gift for Margaret*. My mother had won a prize – a Boots No.7 Protect and Perfect Skincare Travel Kit. Nothing about my entry. While pleased for her, I began to fall into the slough that always follows a rejection. Then I remembered; I'd used a different email address for my own story, so as not to cause confusion. I was away at the time, and could only access this other address from my home computer. Again, I forgot all about it. After I'd been back for a couple of days, I remembered again. I opened the other email account. *Heathrow 70 Stories: Qantas Prize Winner*. I'd only gone and won the top bloody prize, return flights on Qantas to Sydney for two with accommodation! On an Airbus A380, the biggest ever airliner, a double-decker I'd never flown on!

I didn't credit it at first. It must be a scam. Someone must have somehow found out I'd entered and be trying to phish my personal details. My wife helped to convince me it was real – it all looked legit, and was from a proper *heathrow.com* email address, but I didn't really believe it until I saw my story there on the webpage with my own photograph. It was taken from the place I sat waiting for my flight to ORK in the new Queen's Terminal, quite possibly super-imposing an image of myself sitting on the terrace of the old Queen's Building forty years before, holding my binoculars rather than a mochaccino. I suppose that's one of the things the judges liked.

I hadn't given the piece the title *To The Queen's Terminal*. In fact, I'm not sure I gave it a title at all, and they'd changed all the punctuation – I wouldn't have put an exclamation mark in the first line, 'In the 70s, my brother and I were plane spotters!'. Planespotters is also one word, as far as I'm concerned. But so what – my story had won me a trip to Australia! And that *is* my exclamation mark.

/

I call my mother every Sunday to see how she is, our regular agenda items being:

- The Weather
- Football Results
- Horseracing
- Family Gossip

And on this occasion, there was also some Any Other Business in the form of the Heathrow Stories competition result.

"You know that piece you asked me to type up and enter in that competition?"

"Yes…"

"Well, you won a prize."

"Oh, did I? What did I win?"

"You won a Boots Skincare Travel Set."

"Ooh, that's nice. Did you enter?"

"Yes, I did."

"And did you win anything?"

"Yes, I did. A trip to Australia."

Maternal pride and envy battled for supremacy. Maternal pride got the upper hand, just.

After twenty-four hours of exhilaration, some of the practical considerations kicked in. The trip was for just one week – in fact, after the day and night of flying at each end, there were only five nights of staying in Sydney. It was a set time – departure on the last day of May 2017. It was economy class; I don't want to sound fussy, but we had been to Australia once before and swore to ourselves if we ever went back we'd save up for business or first or premium economy or super-duper lux, whatever. It's a killer, especially if you're six foot-ish – me just over, my wife just under. We weren't allowed to upgrade either. For those reasons, she decided she didn't want to come. So who *would* accompany me?

I went through a list. My early partner in aviation crime, my brother. He declined, for the same reasons – too far, too little time there. My best mate Paddy, of the JFK guitar. No – he'd have to come over from Prague, his current roost, and money was tight. My mother – after all, I'd never have known about the competition without her. But she felt at her age it would be too demanding. I even asked my singing teacher, we seemed to get on well enough. But I think we both knew that would be inappropriate. She certainly did, from her pleasant enough but somewhat stiff reply. It ultimately went to a friend.

But in the event neither of us went to Sydney. I'd previously been selected as the Liberal Democrat parliamentary candidate for my home constituency and then, shortly before my planned trip, Theresa May called a general election.

Suffice it to say, I did not get the seat. Even if there is another election soon, which seems possible, I doubt I'll stand again. Quite apart from whether I want to or not (and perhaps more significantly whether my wife wants me to or not), late in the campaign someone found out about my 'trust fund kid' background, and whatever my sentiments on the matter, I have to admit offshore tax havens and centre-left politics don't really mix.

In the end, the friend I'd given the ticket to wasn't on that plane coming back to London either. She hadn't even been on the plane out to Sydney. She was taken ill the day before departure from Heathrow. So we both missed the trip, her partner going out on his own!

I may not have been able to go to Sydney or win the Lib Dem seat, but it did kickstart this book. I'll happily take that.

CAT

I'm on a plane again. But this time it's not family stuff, flying to a corner of Europe to conduct a fire sale or flog an ailing business from under the nose of some poor old sod. No, this time the flight's for my benefit. A flight of fancy?

Perhaps. I'm going to Sicily for a musical retreat, and I'm hoping to do some writing while I'm out here – I can't imagine there is anything my father would be less likely to do. But then I am not him. And he won't be able to reach me up in the remote hills below the shadow of Mount Etna.

It's more difficult for him to contact me now anyway, even when I'm at home, because I've stopped receiving faxes from him. I know fathers and sons don't have umbilical cords but pulling out the power cable from the fax machine felt pretty much like cutting the cord between us. It accelerated his rage; I'd had the effrontery to sever the means of communication between us! I see everything more clearly now, and I realise there's no such word as 'reciprocal' in my father's vocabulary. Everything leads one way, the way that benefits him. It reminds me of the recalibration after the public reveal of his infidelity; although he'd broken my mother's heart he fully expected her to readjust to the new circumstances. He would keep coming home on the very rare occasion it suited him, and she would put up with him doing whatever suited him for the majority of the time. She didn't buy that one, and I failed him in my refusal to sell it to her. I'll never be the person he wants me to be, a mere adjunct to him, a weapon in his armoury.

We're twenty minutes out of Catania, which has one of the most spectacular approaches of any airport anywhere. Having escaped the European mainland passing over the French Riviera, the plane is entombed in vivid blue above and below, until the crystals of Corsica and Sardinia pass below. Descending, the fishing boats become distinguishable from the white horses. Squeezing past the rugged peaks at the centre of the island, the biggest one of all suddenly blocks the way, Etna, snowcapped even in May. The pilot treats it with healthy respect and swings the plane out over the sea, ensuring the final approach is smooth and flat over the water.

My flight lands a few minutes early which is a plus. I sort out my hire car and am in good time to meet Talia, my singing teacher and the one running this musical retreat. All I need is one of those white card signs to hold with her name scrawled on it. I only have to wait a few minutes and she comes through all smiles; I guess it's nice being met at an airport when your suitcase is almost bigger than you. Well, she is here for a month, as opposed to my hand-baggage-only stay.

Within minutes of her coming through customs we are in the car driving out onto the autostrada, heading inland. After about half an hour, we take an exit; the roads get narrower and narrower, more and more windy. Despite being too tight to fork up for the satnav option, I make only one small error, which I quickly spot and rectify, and get us there safe and sound. Talia is impressed; I may be a novice singer, but I can navigate.

On the first night of my musical retreat, I sleep better than I have for years, not waking until 10am. No fear of late-night red-wine-fuelled faxes from my father telling me how inadequate I am! No *rumble-click-click* from the machine downstairs just as I am drifting off!

Part of my newfound freedom is down to my recently achieved financial independence. We have sold our house and downsized – my father is no longer my 'bread and butter'. His crony, who had investigated me for potential art and jewellery theft, had warned me I should sell my house, no doubt knowing I was about to be cut off, but his threat evolved into an opportunity as we realised that to sell it would help liberate us, liberate me, to do things like this.

Disinheritance. It's a price worth paying, especially as I never put much stock by it in the first place.

I have a two-hour lesson with Talia every day, and I can feel my confidence and my voice improving. I do have time to write, and I find the words coming to me quickly. I find a special place to go – a large rock half way down the field below the *fattoria* to lean on while I sit and scribble. My back to the rock like my back to my father. I've broken down the rock of him: still pebbles to negotiate, and maybe slip on a little as they scree downhill, but mostly they roll harmlessly away and I can start to navigate my own path.

Although I'm the only retreat participant, it turns out to be much more social than first impressions suggested. There are other people coming and going: musicians, artists, friends. Hospitality and homemade bay leaf tea are always on tap. I am at home here more than I am in any of my father's many houses. I can laugh and chat freely. Well, as freely as I can with my stuttering Italian. No 'networking' at trade shows, no boardroom bullshitting now.

My week comes to an end, and it's time to drive to Catania airport and catch the plane back to Gatwick. As I'm travelling with only hand baggage, I've had to be careful with the contraband I can return with. I have 100ml of home-produced olive oil which I've dispensed into an empty regulation-size shampoo bottle. I have bay leaves from the hillside. I have Sicilian biscuits, no issue with customs there. And I have a small jar of local marmalade, which along with the olive oil, I've secreted into my clear cosmetic bag with my lotions and potions.

On the last evening at Raddusa, we climbed to the top of a prominent rock looming over the town with a friend of the host family. Looking down over the town and the infinite plain beyond, I must have looked a little wistful. A friend spotted this and, with her limited English and some helpful translation from Talia, she asked if I was 'anxious or relaxed'. I said relaxed, and mostly I was, albeit a little apprehensive about going home. Probably both would have been the correct answer. Probably still is. I'm not sure I'll ever be anything different. But that's who I am, sensitive and speccy, not an extra iron limb attached to another man.

(Disclaimer: I still like cars and planes. The fuel runs too deep within my veins.)

LGW

I'm using satnav to find the pre-flight Gatwick hotel ahead of our early morning departure. I'm really a map man and sure enough the satnav lets me down, taking me to a residential cul-de-sac close to the airport perimeter road. I revert to common sense and soon locate the hotel. I check in and get organised. I've done the research and where I've chosen seems pretty close to the terminal. I should even be able to walk over for an evening meal.

But I hadn't reckoned on it all having gone a bit LA – fly-overs and underpasses and no pavement or pedestrians. Running across dual carriageways and scaling fences in the dark? Not happening. I establish that there is a shuttle bus to the terminal, but it'll cost me £3 and go all round the houses. I give in and have a bland hotel dinner in the bland hotel restaurant.

Oh well. I'm getting up at six in the morning anyway. Which I do, and then have no choice about the shuttle bus, with all my luggage. We're doing the sensible thing and arriving the full three prescribed hours before take-off. I meet my sister and one brother for breakfast; the other one quite understandably didn't want to join in this lunatic adventure. We're flying, initially to the States, with our precious cargo.

During my election campaign, my father's long-term partner finally succumbed to her Alzheimer's and quietly passed away. Since that time, her ashes have sat in Spain, where she died. She had no relatives, having been an only child and then hooking up with my father, who already had four children, thank you. She left a wish for her ashes to be spread in Florida, out on the ranch they had there. We've decided to oblige because we're heading that way anyway, with ashes of our urn. Own, I mean.

Because just a few months later my father's died too. And he wanted his ashes spread in the Caribbean. So now the three of us are playing pass the parcel with the two urns. Taking your baggage with you has a whole new meaning.

/

Gatwick was our departure point on one of those early family holidays abroad when they had to sweep snow off the wings. With brooms. The airport used to be second on our planespotting hitlist after Heathrow though it was a pain to get to by public transport, despite being only thirty miles as the helicopter flies. We'd have to cadge a lift or do the long walk to get the Windsor bus, then a tandem of those Green Line Coaches – the 747 to Heathrow and the 727 between the two airports. What with the changes, the journey took a good three hours, leaving a thin sandwich filling of planespotting between the thick slices of travel.

We had to go to both airports because different airlines and planes visited, ones we would never see at Heathrow. Bear in mind the ultimate goal for a planespotter is to see every aircraft in the world, an impossible task of course, but if we were going to do our job properly, we had to at least try.

For the flying public, Gatwick played second fiddle to Heathrow and still does, with its single runway and greater distance from Central London. The bigger, richer airlines would pay the higher landing fees that Heathrow could command, leaving Gatwick to the national carriers of developing countries and charter companies. Gatwick also had its own 'General Aviation' terminal catering for the visiting flocks of business jets and other private aircraft.

Despite the slog of getting there the effort was worth it, because we'd always come home with a bigger hit of numbers than we'd get from a quick fix at Heathrow. Quality as well as quantity – exotic South American and African airliners with their vivid liveries.

Towards the end of our planespotting tenure, we did more than look at planes, we actually flew on one. The 'Viscount Preservation Trust' organised a flight not on a Vickers Viscount but on an entirely different old plane, a Douglas DC-6. This was a propeller airliner from the 1950s and, as it says on the blurb, by 1977 there were just three still in European passenger service. The plane can only have been some twenty or so years old, but it was by then already a relic of flight's propeller-driven ice age before the roaring 70s of the big jets.

We were airborne for an hour, on our way to nowhere, skimming the South Downs with the aching drone of the big old props. At least there were four of them.

They're still de-icing the wings. Gatwick does seem to get more than its fair share of wintry weather. A few years back we were almost stranded in Cork, days before Christmas, but scraped our way onto a flight to Gatwick on Christmas Eve. Due to some freakish combination of the bad weather and air traffic restrictions, we had to fly the last fifty miles at pylon-dusting height; doing this in a hundred-ton airliner you really know you're flying. It was stunning to see the whiteout below in the late afternoon winter sun, low clouds scuttling beneath and through us. The first landing attempt was aborted, a cotton wool roll of snowy cloud obscuring the runway at the crucial moment, but with the strong gusts it had passed through before we ended our next lap and we touched down through the empty pocket. Proper piloting.

I'm in debt to the airport too for my stand-up comedy persona, Adrian Gatwick, planespotter extraordinaire. Sounds better than Adrian Heathrow, doesn't it? I think I made nine appearances, mostly in the so-called guest spot, shorthand for unpaid. And that meant being up first, dealing with an audience yet to find their seats and their sense of humour. I dressed the part, wearing an anorak (of course), binoculars round my neck and sometimes with air band radio in hand.

I made observations about the world from a planespotter's point of view – Adrian's main interest in a world leaders' summit in London would be the number of presidential aircraft in town. I'd take out my airband radio and fiddle with the knobs. I'd look through my binoculars at audience members sitting at the back. I'd enlighten the crowd with amusing insights into the world of aviation, explaining such things as stacking. Yes, I wasn't immune to the occasional double entendre. For those still lost in the cloud, stacking is what aeroplanes do when they're queuing up at different flight levels prior to landing.

My act went down alright, I was even invited back to some places. One time when it wasn't actually going particularly well, a young woman in the audience nonetheless found me hilarious, laughing so raucously that other members wondered whether she was a plant.

Maybe I should have stuck with it, but I didn't have sufficient confidence to persevere, and Adrian hung up his binoculars. I did love that brief interlude as a stand-up though; while I was being someone else, I was actually being more 'me'. Yes, Adrian Gatwick was a more genuine reflection of my true character than the attempted proto-businessman I felt my father wanted me to be, though it took me decades to come to terms with this. It was never something I would ever achieve anyway; ironically, on the occasions I did excel in something – getting into the LSE when he'd never been to university, winning writing prizes – he displayed jealousy towards me. My greatest crime was daring to be and express myself rather than being a mere adjunct of his own increasingly bloated personality.

/

Now, they've finished spraying the wings and we're ready for take-off on our long transatlantic flight. I settle into my seat and get out my book. It's written by a famous writer I used to go clubbing with. We drifted apart in the 80s when I got my steady job and my steady girlfriend while he carried on partying. I bumped into him again a few years ago, but he treated me like an autograph hunter. I told him I'd started doing some writing myself and he replied, "I always say to people when they tell me that – 'Prose? Leave it to the pros'". Still, I read his book, and grudgingly admire his skill.

It's late afternoon when the Florida coast appears on our righthand side. "Twenty minutes to landing," the pilot says; we'll be early. We sweep round towards it. The peninsular is so narrow here you can see the Gulf of Mexico beyond, the swampy Everglades the only land between, the destination for Ursula's ashes. Briefly we head towards them, by-passing the airport. Then we pull a steep 180 and commence finals over the freeway lattice below.

It's been the perfect flight.

PLS

There are times during this bizarre odyssey when I just have to laugh. We're back at Fort Lauderdale airport (IATA code FLL for the record) – me, my sister and a brother. We've scattered one cask of ashes, Ursula's. Now we just have one urn with us, my father's. I'm amazed we've got as far as we have without any serious challenge, all the way to Florida from Gatwick with the remains of two people in our hand luggage.

Now we're on the last leg, just one short flight before we can disperse the remaining half of our precious cargo into the sea. We're all on the same flight, but my brother booked separately and he rushes through the check-in process leaving me and my sister (and the ashes) in his wake. Our transition through customs doesn't go so smoothly. Firstly, the automatic machine doesn't like our UK passports, and we have to join the long queue which should really just have a big electronic sign above it which says 'Awkward Customers'. Finally we reach the desk. We've decided to say nothing at this stage about the contents of our hand baggage, we'll save that for customs. I help my sister hoist her massive hold bag onto the scales. I wonder if she's got someone else's corpse in it for good measure. It's way over the limit and she can't move anything into her hand luggage because that's full. With the urn.

We're doing a fine job of being *really* awkward passengers and making everyone else in the queue wait even longer. I ask her if she's got anything heavier than the shoes in her bag – any books, for example? A lightbulb illuminates and she extracts some three-in-one whodunit hardback, which immediately gets the weight under the limit! Or close enough that the exasperated ground staff give it the nod anyway.

On to the security scanner. We come clean about the ashes, ready to dig out some paperwork if it gets awkward. But no, the mere mention of mortality provokes sympathetic smiles, and though we have to wait an age for the special tray resembling a big waffle iron that ashes go on to pass through the machine (who knew there was such a thing?) nobody gives us a hard time and we're finally reuniting with our brother in the departure lounge, the ashes at our side.

When I started writing all this, I couldn't contemplate he'd actually be dead by the end of it. I didn't realise how much of my life he'd permeated until he wasn't there any longer, and the sky was calm but undeniably void. When you finally stop fighting against something, you'd think it would be a relief, and it is, but there's an undeniable emptiness too.

/

In what turned out to be his last few months, if anyone tried to phone him to see how he was, invariably his girlfriend Mandy answered, and he could be heard ranting in the background, "No visitors, no visitors!" His globetrotting had diminished but he maintained the bones of his international annual schedule – winters split between Florida and the Caribbean, summers mostly Spain with a month or so at Mandy's flat on the Wirral, which I suspect he paid for. And that's where he'd been when his frail health had finally given up on him. The damp climate had done him no good, summer not having bothered to make an appearance in the north-west of England, and his weak chest had picked up its final infection.

I had seen him before the end, but it hadn't been straightforward. His 'no visitors' rants hadn't just been a show; my cousin had turned up at his villa in Spain shortly before my father left for the UK and had this brief conversation:

"Hello, Uncle David."

"What are you doing here?"

"I came to see you."

"Well now you have, so you can go."

The wounded lion not wanting to show his fallibility, maybe.

When he'd been taken ill, I'd decided to head up the next morning to the Arrowe Park Hospital just outside Birkenhead, if only for my own benefit. Even though we were no longer on speaking terms, I had loved him once – maybe I still did in a perverse, reluctant way – and if he was going to die, I wanted to see him before the end. If he wanted me to go away again, fine, but at least I'd have tried. My brother wasn't so sure. "He keeps telling us he doesn't want to see us – if that's how he wants it, then fine."

By the next morning my brother had mellowed and we'd agreed to meet at a motorway services outside Birmingham and share the driving from there. It was raining when we got to Birkenhead, but of course we parked in the free car park furthest away from the hospital. Maybe we were following the family tight-arse typecast, maybe we were being indignant about the money-spinning paying car park scam, or maybe we were just putting off the moment.

The hospital was modern and crisply clean, an aura of friendly efficiency penetrating the inevitable mile-long corridors. Nonetheless, we found him easily enough. There was our father, propped up and not looking like dying anytime soon after all. Here he was, not long off his private jet, in the corner of a packed noisy ward in an NHS hospital.

But he didn't tell us to go home again. He smiled. And he spoke. Or tried to – the words wouldn't really come out, and we struggled to translate his hoarse whisper, though his pleasure that we'd come was clear enough. He seemed genuinely surprised that we'd made the effort, after everything he'd done to try to alienate us. "What, you've come all the way up from Somerset? This morning?" he croaked, and I found I was glad I had.

Each utterance tired him, but they continued to come at intervals – he held up a hand and challenged my brother to arm wrestle him. He had to tell us how pretty the nurses were. He complimented the food. After about quarter of an hour though he was played out, and the arrival of medics to do something with tubes provided an opportune moment to slip away.

Downstairs in the café we spoke with his girlfriend and her sister about next steps. My father's dubious national and marital status were presenting challenges. He was The Man Who Fell to Earth – no NHS number, no UK abode… and who were they, the sisters, these two women half his age at his bedside?

Well, they were his personal nurses, or at least that's how they'd described themselves to get as far as they had. That said, to the credit of our beloved NHS, unanswered questions weren't allowed to obstruct his care, and it was quickly apparent Mandy had got him into hospital just in time, and that night they'd saved his life. His chest had been so weak that his heart wasn't getting sufficient stimulus to pump the blood around his body.

Our arrival provided an essential ingredient, next of kin, and we started planning (finally, like it or not, he had to depend on someone else). He and Mandy wanted to get him back to Spain, where the hot dry air could soothe his aching lungs. I set about finding an air ambulance to fly him from Liverpool back to Malaga.

All seemed to be going well, the tough old goat fought off that round of infection with the benefit of first-class care, and he went into a nearby nursing home to recuperate, pending the day he was deemed strong enough for the flight.

From then on, we took it in turns to provide back-up for his girlfriend, with a doctor cousin filling in the gaps. Every time I'd see my father he had just one message for me – I had to get him back to Spain, because he'd die if he stayed where he was. I researched the air ambulance options. He fixated on September 2nd, the date his original air charter had been booked for his return. He made me show him the quotation for the new flight. He'd wait until Mandy was out of the room before pleading with me. It had become clear she knew he wasn't going to live and now wanted him to die on her home patch. She and I began to row. I could understand all the reasons for him to stay where he was, but if Spain was what he wanted...

The next time I visited, he was having a good day. He was delighted to see both my companions, my wife and Lewis the dog. In his Dallas world where he was Head Honcho, he'd always seen my wife as some sort of queen in waiting. She was supposed to love him more than me, though she gave him no grounds to entertain such a notion. On one occasion, he'd even called her 'his chatelaine', when we had the estate in France. Maybe all the women he knew were supposed to love him more than their own partners. Unfortunately I think some of them did.

At the home, there was a barbecue going on downstairs out on the terrace, and my father wanted some of the action. Mandy had taken advantage of our presence to take a break, fair enough with all she'd been doing, so we were his escort. The nurses got him ready and loaded him into a wheelchair, then we all crammed into a lift. Let's get the party started.

Most of the other residents were already arranged in ripples from a centre where some form of entertainment was clearly imminent. Lewis the dog loved the idea of a barbecue and the residents loved Lewis. Someone offered my father a drink and he asked for a glass of red wine. Yay!

It turned out red wine was not available, but to my surprise a glass of rosé was produced, which he gladly accepted. He took a sip and it made him cough, but he wasn't giving up on it. We sat there waiting for something to happen; nothing did, and he was getting cold. An extra blanket was requisitioned, and that helped briefly, but I could see he was still cold, and he consented to my suggestion we take him back upstairs before any food or entertainment had been provided. He'd had a change of scenery for twenty minutes and a few sips of wine. After those exertions, he wanted to rest, so we left him for the day and found our dog-friendly hotel.

The beach was a short walk away and we cleared our heads and stretched our legs across the infinite sands, the sea almost lost at their margin. We'd chanced upon the European Sand Buggy Championships, and in the far distance their sails fluttering in multicolour semaphore in the late afternoon sun, flashes of light and freedom beyond the oppressive nursing home and his impending departure.

We returned to his bedside the next day; it wasn't such a good one. Again he implored me to get him back to Spain. Mandy was there too, and I asked him in front of her if that was really what he wanted. We ended up having an almighty and undignified row in front of him – it's a relief that the details have already receded into a vague memory. The outcome though was that he said in front of all of us that no, he didn't want to go back to Spain, he would stay where he was.

In some ways it was a godsend. It relieved me of the conflict I felt between doing what was best for him and doing what he wanted.

Shortly after that, the doctor arrived on her rounds. She confirmed his vital signs had slid since her last visit, and didn't give him more than a few days. She said the flight would probably kill him. I knew that but it wasn't the point. Nevertheless it felt like the referee blowing the whistle after a particularly fraught and demanding match.

I went back in to see my father after I'd spoken with the doctor. Mandy was at his side, in tears. I kissed him, said goodbye and told him I loved him. That was the truth, I did. Even after all the anguish, I couldn't help loving my father. He smiled back weakly and lightly took my hand. We all knew what this farewell meant.

It was my sister's turn to visit next. My father was reasonably okay the day she arrived, but she phoned the next morning with another of those 'you'd better get up here' calls. He'd had a bad night; he was in pain for the first time, and they'd given him morphine. Now he was restful but for the first time not really making sense in his fleeting awakenings.

I'd told my wife this time I wasn't going to drop everything and go. Not because I didn't expect the worst, but because I didn't feel the need to go. I was comfortable with our last encounter.

Very soon there was such a phone call. He'd slipped quietly away with my sister holding one hand and Mandy holding the other.

/

As the wheels kiss the tarmac, the shadow plane shrinks away and we're left with the reality of disembarking with our special delivery to its final resting place. To our surprise we skip through customs and immigration in the small terminal, and the local housekeeper Mickey is out there in the heat to meet us, in the sort of beaten-up 4x4 that's essential for the island roads.

We ask her about the damage in the wake of Hurricane Irma; I'd seen pictures of the whole airport several fathoms underwater though it's hard to imagine now, the runways fading out into dusty dry scrub.

"It's still bad," she tells us. "Some people haven't yet got their water and electricity back, especially in the poorer parts of the island."

We soon see for ourselves just how bad it still is some three months after the storm hit. Road signs and telegraph poles are a giant's matchsticks discarded along the kerb. Cables snake off them into the unkempt verges, themselves shrapnelled with rubble. Signposts hang empty, or with fluttering shreds of information rendered useless. Roofs hang off buildings, and there's construction work going on – or not going on – everywhere. The Turks & Caicos authorities have been playing down just how bad it is, because other islands, like the Caymans, are even worse, and they don't want to lose the already endangered tourist trade that's still coming their way.

Irma hit the same time our father died. Several wags commented that it wasn't Irma at all, it was Hurricane David, my father wreaking his last trail of havoc as he departed from this world.

We reach the house. It looks worse off for the hurricane, but it was scruffy already, even though it had been supposedly redecorated when he bought it a decade earlier. It had been a backpacker hostel called Back of Beyond, for good reason. It's on the less fashionable side of the island, away from the beaches of Grace Bay. I stumbled on a Trip Advisor ad recently telling me they've been voted best in the world – is that best in the world where the hotels are still standing? But our side is also the more protected side, and actually the damage appears superficial – the screens and awnings shredded, a few shutters splintered to pieces.

We check out the rooms, which are all accessed from outside at the back of the house, showing its heritage as a hostel. We're trying to find ones with both working air conditioning and running water. There aren't many. My brother decides to sleep in my father's room. Rather him than me, it still has all my father's clothes, books and paraphernalia in it – a lifetime's supply of vintage hearing aids, enough little packets of tissues and wet wipes to stock a transatlantic airliner.

The following day we scout out the venue where we're having a small memorial service for him – it's a restaurant with a large covered-but-open space at the back. Then having negotiated the remaining planks on the gangway potholed by the hurricane, we meet the captain of the boat that's going to take us out to spread the ashes. This boat

by comparison to l

father's captain – n

its use for this final

When we'd sp

the Everglades fro

A warm windless

moment with a s

warns us of wor

weather, but rain

be a 9am phone (

Next mornii

tourists come fo

But the call com

we'll be staying

and crowd onto

baton.

As we head

three yachts flu

the chop, chop

part and the su

sea, and it take:

from his first o

of us on the b(

drop anchor, a

it in turns to sl

wind suddenl

possible of th

father the last

Next mc

to the US ma

in the heat i

island. The ¡

pilot slams the jet

the calm water w

us. We climb stee

Mission comp

engines onto full throttle. We pass directly over
here my father's ashes float and sparkle back at
ly into the blue air, no turbulence.
leted, according to his wishes.

Final
Approach

I'm going to an airport today but I'm not planning on flying anywhere. No, this is more like a day-trip pilgrimage to pay my respects to all the dead planes – and my dead father. Before Covid, climate emergency and corporate collapse I thought nothing of getting on a plane most weeks, and mostly that travel would have something to do with my father. While he was still alive, planes were a constant, criss-crossing our disjointed, dysfunctional lives. Childhood planespotter, wondering if he might be coming home on one of the prehistoric jets thundering in to land over our heads, to adult globetrotter, looking after his countless properties and business interests in nine different countries. Taking the jumpseat when he graduated to his own private jet.

I miss my dad, bastard though he was, and I miss planes; visiting an airfield and looking at them will have to suffice. So I'm off to Kemble, the closest we have in the UK to an aviation boneyard where old airliners go to die, less than a two-hour drive away. I couldn't admit it, maybe I didn't even know it, but it was always all about him.

It's the perfect day to visit. It's clear but not icy, the roads are fine and it should be good photographing weather. I leave soon after breakfast, heading north east, and sure enough the A303, the infamous trunk road past Stonehenge down to the South West of England where I now live quietly, is emptier than at any time since lockdown.

I turn on the radio. I want BBC 6 Music for Lauren Laverne's company but my system's decided to wipe itself clean – no channels. I hit 'Scan', and the first one which pops up is Smooth Somerset. They're playing Michael Jackson; that will do on this sunny, carefree morning. Then Culture Club, early Elton John and Sade. I thought the 6 Music playlist was getting more yoof, but maybe I'm getting more smooth, ain't that the truth.

Actually, maybe I'm not getting more smooth. I have a lovely drive for an hour until a road rage incident with a lorry driver.

He tries to force me into oncoming traffic along the confusing single/dual/single carriageway ring road around Trowbridge. Having seen my death approaching me in the solid form of another lorry, at the next lights I leap out of my car and swear at the first lorry driver, probably frightening the woman in the 4x4 alongside.

This is not the person I want to be.

I'm supposed to be *chilled*, especially after a couple of years of counselling, and the whole point of this journey is to have a *chilled* day for my own benefit. After all the stress, strain and heartache, I've survived and, unlike others in similar situations, I haven't succumbed to alcohol or other addictions.

I regain my equilibrium and drive on, steadily. The lorry driver has backed off. I guess being a sweary beardy six-foot-three apparition weighing fifteen stone, I did look quite the crazy man. I arrive at Kemble, now Cotswold Airport, IATA code GBA, without further incident.

My father died four years ago. My charming, abusive, chameleon of a father. Everything about him was complicated or 'complex', an excuse he used whenever it served a purpose. Even in death it's still complicated, as if his interfering tendrils are spidering up from his grave. Four years on and we're still dealing with his probate. The registrar where this 'complex' high-net-worth individual was domiciled – the Turks and Caicos Islands, home to Rolling Stone Keith Richard, among others – hasn't yet granted probate.

I went from being his first ever passenger in his flimsy little helicopter to arranging the air ambulance to take him on his final flight. Of course he went and died before he could be trolleyed on board. Typical.

I can see even as I approach the airfield that it hasn't been a wasted journey. Parked next to the main road are a line of TAP Air Portugal Airbuses, with a redundant British Airways Boeing

747 lurking at their tail. That's a Jumbo Jet to those who aren't card-carrying aviation addicts. The problem is, there's nowhere to stop for my first photo – the authorities obviously don't want kerb crawlers like me cluttering up the verges, which are littered with double yellow lines. No matter, I pull into a wide access road opposite; it's still yellow tinged, but there's room enough to park up for a minute with my hazards on. I run across the busy road taking my life in my hands and rush the first snap on my phone, using my height to overcome the six-foot-high barbed wire.

I pull up close to the control tower and the airfield's AV8 restaurant with a view to having lunch before I cruise the perimeter to hunt down every winged beast. The car park and the open terrace in front of the café are full of like-minded people – there's clearly still a small army of anorak-clad, binocular-laden aviation enthusiasts out there. Not kids though; they're mostly blokes my age. I suppose it is midweek term-time.

The restaurant doesn't inspire confidence. Good job I brought supplies in case it was closed. I settle down in the car with a ham sandwich, made with my own home-baked bread. My windscreen faces straight out onto the apron, and I raise my head when I hear an engine powering up.

It's a helicopter and I manage to get a shot of it as it lifts off over a hangar emblazoned with the legend 'Freedom Aviation'. There's a concept that deserves some deconstruction. Aviation can certainly buy you a little freedom if you've got enough money. Freedom from the pull of the earth at the most base level; freedom to escape Little Britain for a few hours, maybe longer if you charter a jet to an island paradise. Ultimately the freedom is transitory. Real freedom lies elsewhere.

As it takes off in front of the hangar, the helicopter is a frail grasshopper of a machine; it's hard to comprehend that it can defy gravity. I can't watch it ascend without thinking of Father.

That flight with him, the novice chopper pilot, in an even more elemental tangle of tubes and glass than this contraption. It's a miracle I'm here. As well as all the grief he gave me, I benefitted from his luck.

But now, sandwich finished, I have work to do. There are rows and rows of airliner husks dotted over the large terrain; they're a colourful clutch, evocative of a happier, shinier incarnation of aviation where every aeroplane might be approaching a sun-drenched beach, ready to spill out laughing passengers in sunhats and sandals onto the tarmac.

All I can do is take a long-range photograph of their anonymous silhouettes in the late afternoon sun. It's a fitting end to my day; the sun will rise on them again, but it will be an empty purposeless sun as these planes will never again rise from the runway and head off into its heart.

I imagine I'm not sitting in my car about to drive home, but sitting in one those aircraft. I'm on a plane to nowhere. I'm determined to buckle up and enjoy the flight.

ACKNOWLEDGMENTS

I will launch into this by thanking Katie Isbester and Alexander Green at Claret Press who saw the blue sky beyond the turbulence and took on the challenge of *Final Approach* – and me!

There are many others who helped me deliver my complicated flight plan. Thank you to Christina Dunhill at City Lit who saw something of a writer in the businessman doing evening classes and took me under her wing. Thanks to Emma Sawyer, Reuben Lane, Mia Farlane, Alan McCormick and Anne Bennett who gave me valuable advice in the departure lounge.

Thank you also to Mike Ormsby and Ursula and James Cornish for helping to fuel my itinerary. Thank you to Aki Schilz, Joe Sedgwick, Nelima Begum and Julia Forster at The Literary Consultancy.

But I am most grateful to those who have flown through the turbulence with me – my mother Margaret, my sister Alison, my brothers Stephen and Daniel and more than anyone, my wife Lynn for enduring the journey with me.

I dedicate this book to my planespotting partner in crime, who's also gone straight now, my brother Stephen Blackburn.

ABOUT THE AUTHOR

 Mark, the oldest of four children, arrived in London during the heyday of punk to study at the LSE. Sundry abortive attempts at stardom followed: a stand-up comedian, actor and musician.

After a successful career as a shoeseller, Mark left London and now lives in Somerset, England, doing what he loves best - writing. Dame Margaret Drabble selected Mark as runner-up in the Interact Ruth Rendell Short Story Prize, saying how much she loved and related to his story, *The Wall*. He was also shortlisted for the 2022 TLC Pen Factor Pitch Prize.

Mark has had other short stories, poetry, nonfiction publishing in print and online. He is the author of two children's books.

When he isn't writing, he may well be found under the bonnet of an old car trying to coax it back to life on a classic car rally.

Facebook: https://facebook.com/mdhblackburn
Twitter: https://twitter.com/markblackburn
Instagram: https://instagram.com/mdhblackburn

Claret Press

GREAT STORYTELLING DOESN'T JUST ENTERTAIN, IT ENERGISES

Claret Press' mission is simple: we publish engrossing books which engage with the issues of the day. So we publish across a range of genres, both fiction and nonfiction. From award-winning page-turners to eye-opening travelogues, from captivating historical fiction to insightful memoirs, there's a Claret Press book for you.

To keep up to date about the going-ons at Claret Press, including book launches, zoom talks and other events, sign up to our newsletter through our website at **www.claretpress.com.**

You can also find us through Instagram **@claretpress** Twitter **@ClaretPress** and YouTube **@claretpress**